YOUR ULTIMATE RETIREMENT ADVENTURE: FUN THINGS TO DO IN YOUR POST-WORK LIFE

LEISURE PURSUITS AND METHODS TO STAY ACTIVE, EASILY BUILD CONNECTIONS, AND DISCOVER A WIDE VARIETY OF ACTIVITIES WITHOUT BREAKING THE BANK

ALAN TURNER

INTRODUCTION

When the doors to my office closed behind me for the last time, I felt an unexpected surge of freedom mixed with a hint of uncertainty. Retirement had come earlier than planned, thanks to a sweeping reorganization at my company. As I stepped into the brisk air that autumn morning, I realized my professional life had ended. Still, another chapter was waiting to be written, filled with potential for personal growth, exploration, and joy. Early retirement wasn't the end; it was a vibrant new beginning.

This book is not your typical guide to retirement. It's a unique resource crafted for you, the modern retiree, who sees the silver years not as a slow wind-down but as a time rich with opportunities.

It's for those of you who are just stepping into retirement and those who have been enjoying this phase for a while but are seeking more. Here, you will find not just activities but gateways to new experiences that are fulfilling and fun. This is a fresh, dynamic approach to living a life full of vibrancy and enthusiasm post-career.

What sets this guide apart is its embrace of technology as an integral part of the retirement adventure. From mastering basic computer skills to navigating social media platforms and using apps like WhatsApp and Facebook, technology is not just about staying connected—it's about making new connections and discovering passions. This book is designed to be inclusive, considering all budgets, physical abilities, and lifestyles. Whether married or single, with or without children, there's something here for everyone.

As someone who was nudged into early retirement, I understand the mixed emotions that come with this transition. I, too, struggled to find the sense of purpose my work once provided. Through trial and exploration, however, I uncovered a wealth of activities that not only filled my days but also profoundly enriched my life. This book shares those insights and more, offering you practical advice from retirees who have found joy and purpose in their new everyday lives.

Structured to make your journey into retirement as enjoyable as it is meaningful, each chapter in this book is a gateway to different types of activities—physical, social, creative, and intellectual. You'll find stories that inspire, tips that guide, and humor that delights, all designed to make your transition into retirement a truly enriching experience.

There is also a chapter on health and well-being. We all know that aging means changes to our bodies, so it's unrealistic to think life will just be singing and dancing all the time. The tips provided might help you stay happy and healthy for a long time so you can treasure all aspects of your post-work life. Having been a nurse myself and working for decades in the health industry, I decided to include this information as well.

Let this book be your companion as you discover that retirement is indeed an adventure—a time to experiment with new hobbies, deepen existing passions, and meet people who share your interests.

It's a time to redefine yourself outside the confines of job titles and work responsibilities and, more importantly, a chance to write a story that's all your own.

So, take this moment to embrace the adventure that lies ahead. With an open mind and heart, step onto this exciting stage where every day holds the promise of something new. Remember, retirement is not just a break from work; it's a broad horizon waiting to be explored. Let's start this journey!

CHAPTER 1: EMBRACING TECHNOLOGY WITH EASE

D o you remember the first time you tried to ride a bike? The initial wobbles, the inevitable falls, but then, the exhilarating sensation of sailing smoothly on two wheels, wind in your hair, mastering a new skill that once seemed so daunting. Embracing technology in your retirement can feel like learning to ride that bike—challenging at first but incredibly rewarding once you get the hang of it.

I dedicated this chapter to turning what might initially appear to be digital hurdles into manageable steps, starting with one of the most essential tools in today's world: the smartphone. Whether you want to stay connected, manage daily tasks, or explore new hobbies, mastering your mobile device is the first step. Let's ease into this digital adventure together, ensuring you have all the support you need right at your fingertips.

1.1 SMARTPHONES 101 FOR SENIORS: SETTING UP YOUR DEVICE

Choosing the Right Smartphone

Selecting the right smartphone is critical, especially because it can significantly simplify your daily routines and make them more enjoyable. Certain features can make the difference between a phone that feels like a lifeline and one that just causes frustration.

Look for phones with large buttons, clear and vibrant displays, user-friendly visuals and systems, and loud volume capabilities. Models like the Jitterbug Smart3 are specifically designed with seniors in mind, offering a large screen and menu, voice typing features, and a powerful speaker. Similarly, the Samsung Galaxy series provides an 'Easy Mode' with fewer, larger icons and simplified menus, making navigation straightforward.

Even though this might sound like all retirees need special assistance, that is far from the truth! Many younger people use text enlargement or hearing aids, and not everyone ages in the same way. I want this book to include helpful tips for anyone who needs them, regardless of the reason.

Initial Setup and Configuration

Setting up your new smartphone is more manageable than it may seem. Here's a step-by-step guide to get you started:

1. **Inserting the SIM Card**: First, locate the SIM tray on your phone. You might need a small tool or a paper clip to open it. This tool will often be provided with the new phone. Carefully insert the SIM card into the tray, ensuring it fits snugly.
2. **Powering On**: Hold the power button until the screen lights up. The first time you turn on your phone, it will guide you through some setup steps.
3. **Connecting to Wi-Fi**: Look for the SETTINGS icon (often shaped like a gear or cog), tap WI-FI, and then choose your home network. Enter the password, and you are connected to the internet without using your data plan.

Basic Functions and Navigation

Once your phone has been set up, mastering a few essential functions will make a world of difference:

- **Making Calls and Sending Texts**: Tap the PHONE icon to enter the dialer to make calls or tap the MESSAGES app to start texting. You can type your message or use voice dictation if typing is cumbersome.
- **Adjusting Settings**: Back in SETTINGS, you can adjust the brightness of your screen, increase the text size, and change the volume. These adjustments make your phone more comfortable to use throughout the day.
- **Downloading Apps**: Visit the App Store (on iPhones) or Google Play Store (on Androids). Here, you can download apps for everything from weather forecasts to health

tracking. Just type what you're looking for into the search bar, select the app, and tap INSTALL.

<u>Customizing for Accessibility</u>

You can also take advantage of built-in accessibility features:

- **Text Enlargement**: Increase the font size in your settings to make reading more comfortable.
- **Voice Commands**: Use Siri, Google Assistant, or another voice assistant to control your phone with spoken commands. This tool is especially handy for searching the internet, calling contacts, or setting reminders without having to type.
- **Hearing Aid Compatibility**: If you use a hearing aid, many smartphones offer compatibility settings to improve audio clarity.

Understanding and adjusting these features can transform a standard device into a personalized tool that fits seamlessly into your life, making daily interactions enjoyable rather than frustrating. As you become more comfortable with these basics, you'll find that your smartphone is more than just a gadget—it's a gateway to a world of information, assistance, and connectivity. So, take your time, play around with the settings, and explore what your new smartphone can do for you!

1.2 NAVIGATING SOCIAL MEDIA: FACEBOOK, INSTAGRAM, AND MORE FOR BEGINNERS

Imagine sitting in your comfortable living room with a cup of tea by your side as you explore vibrant photos of your grandchildren's latest school play, connect with your college friends, or share your gardening tips with enthusiasts around the globe. This is the power of social media—it brings the world to your fingertips, making it smaller and your life richer. Let's walk through the basics of getting you set up and comfortable on popular platforms like Facebook and Instagram. These tools are not just for the younger generation; they hold wonderful opportunities for connection and exploration that can significantly enhance your retirement.

Creating Social Media Accounts

The first step is setting up your accounts. For platforms like Facebook and Instagram, the process is user-friendly and secure, designed to ensure your comfort and protect your privacy. Start by visiting the social media platform's website or downloading the app from your smartphone's app store. You'll be prompted to enter some basic information like your name, email, or phone number. Choose a strong password that includes a mix of letters, numbers, and symbols to enhance security.

Consider using a Password Manager to generate and store all your passwords securely. These systems create passwords that are impossible to crack, and the Password Manager auto-fills them for you. No need to keep a secret list somewhere with all your passwords!

As you set up your account, you'll also encounter privacy settings. Take a moment to customize these settings according to your comfort level—decide who can see your posts, send you friend requests, or share your content. It's like setting the boundaries of your digital home.

Engaging with Content

Once your account is ready, it's time to dive into the world of social media. Platforms like Facebook and Instagram are bustling with content—from family photos to news articles to hobby groups. Learning how to interact with this content is key.

Tap the HEART or THUMBS-UP icons to 'like' a photo or post. Want to share your thoughts? Tap on the COMMENT icon and type away. Sharing posts you find interesting is just as easy. On Facebook, click SHARE to repost it on your timeline for your friends to see, or click SEND to share it directly with someone via private message.

On Instagram, you can use the PAPER AIRPLANE icon to share posts directly with others or repost your story. Uploading your own content is equally straightforward. Tap CREATE POST or the '+' icon, select a photo or video from your device, add some thoughts about it if you wish, and hit POST. Congratulations, you've just added your own sparkle to the social media universe!

Connecting with Family and Friends

Social media excels in connecting people and can help you stay in touch with family and friends, no matter where they are. Use the SEARCH bar to find people you know. Once you find their profiles, send them a friend request or follow them. Additionally, joining groups can be a fantastic way to engage with communities that share your interests. Whether it's a gardening group, a book club, or a travel enthusiasts' group, these communities offer a space to ask questions, share experiences, and meet new people who have the same passions as you.

Managing Privacy and Notifications

Maintaining a comfortable online experience is vital. Take control of who sees your information by adjusting your privacy settings. Most platforms allow you to make your account private, meaning only people you approve can see your content. Managing notifications is also crucial to ensure your social media usage is manageable. You can customize which activities you receive notifications for and how you receive them, whether through the app, email, or not at all. This way, you keep the joy of staying connected without letting it disrupt your daily life.

Navigating social media can initially seem like learning a new language, but once you become familiar with the basics, it becomes a valuable tool for staying engaged and informed. It's a beautiful digital extension of your social circle, offering new avenues for interaction and learning. Whether watching a live video from a local concert or participating in a global discussion on your favorite classic film, social media brings these experiences to your doorstep or, more accurately, to your fingertips. So, take your time, explore at your own pace, and remember, the digital world is yours to enjoy just as much as the real one!

1.3 VIDEO CHATTING WITH FAMILY: A STEP-BY-STEP GUIDE TO SKYPE AND ZOOM

Imagine the joy of seeing your grandchild blow out their birthday candles, hearing the laughter at a family reunion, or sharing a coffee chat with an old friend—all from the comfort of your living room. Video chatting platforms like Skype and Zoom make these delightful moments possible, no matter the miles between. Let's walk through setting up these applications, making video calls, and some handy tips for ensuring you stay connected with your loved ones in this visually engaging digital age when things don't go as planned.

Installing and Setting Up Apps

Getting started with Skype and Zoom is simpler than you might think. First, you'll need a device with a camera, microphone, and speakers—most smartphones, tablets, or laptops come equipped with these.

To download Skype, visit their website or your device's app store and choose the version that suits your device. Similarly, for Zoom, go to the Zoom website or app store and download the app. Once downloaded, you'll need to create an account.

For Skype, you'll set up a username and password. Zoom requires your email address; you can set your login credentials after verification. Remember to keep your passwords secure yet memorable. Perhaps a significant date or a mix of your favorite numbers and a special word? Once logged in, take a few moments to familiarize yourself with the settings. You can adjust your profile information, explore the layout, and check your video and audio settings to ensure everything is working correctly.

<u>Making and Receiving Video Calls</u>

Now, let's make your first call! On Skype, search for a contact by their Skype name or email, and ADD them to your contacts. Once they accept, select their name from your contact list, then click the VIDEO CAMERA icon to start a video call.

On Zoom, you can start a new meeting by clicking the NEW MEETING button, which turns on your camera and starts a session. To invite family or friends, click PARTICIPANTS, then INVITE, and choose to send an invitation via email or directly through Zoom contacts if they're already users.

Receiving calls is straightforward—answer by clicking the accept button with the CAMERA icon on Skype or JOIN WITH VIDEO on Zoom. Suppose you need to mute your microphone during the call or turn off your camera? In that case, both apps have easily accessible controls, usually located at the bottom of the screen.

This feature can be handy if you need a moment to yourself or if there's background noise you'd like to spare your family from!

Scheduling Meetings and Invitations

One of the great features of Zoom is the ability to schedule meetings in advance, which is particularly useful for organizing family gatherings or regular catch-ups. Go to the MEETINGS tab and select SCHEDULE A NEW MEETING. Choose the date and time, set a meeting password for security, and decide on other settings, like whether participants can join before the host (that's you). You can then send out invitations via email, including all the details your family needs to join the meeting. This way, everyone knows when to log on, and everything is clear. It's like sending out digital invitations to an event, only this event can be joined from anywhere in the world.

Troubleshooting Common Issues

Even with the best setup, technology can have its off days, but don't worry—most issues have simple fixes.

If you're experiencing poor connection quality, first ensure your internet connection is stable. Sometimes, moving closer to your Wi-Fi router can improve the connection.

Audio isn't working? Check that your microphone is not muted and the volume is turned up. In both Skype and Zoom, you can access AUDIO SETTINGS to select the correct microphone and speakers.

If the video is not displaying, ensure the camera is on and the lens isn't covered.

Restarting the app or your device can also resolve many common issues. Remember, a quick internet search can solve more specific problems, or you can contact customer support for help.

Video chats can profoundly enrich your life, allowing you to maintain strong, meaningful connections with those you love, witness essential moments, and share experiences that physical distance would otherwise prevent. With these tools at your fingertips, every call can be an opportunity to create cherished memories, no matter where you or your loved ones are. So, go ahead and try it— dial in, connect, and let the good times roll through your screen!

1.4 INTRODUCTION TO ONLINE SHOPPING: SAFETY TIPS AND TRICKS

Imagine the convenience of having everything from groceries to gardening tools, new novels to knitwear, delivered right to your doorstep. Online shopping offers this convenience and much more, allowing you to explore many products without leaving the comfort of your home.

However, as exciting as clicking through a digital shopping cart can be, navigating the e-commerce world safely and smartly is crucial. Let's walk through identifying trustworthy retailers, making secure purchases, protecting your personal information, and handling returns effectively.

<u>Choosing Reliable Online Stores</u>

The internet is bustling with online stores, and while many offer great products and services, some exist to scam unsuspecting shoppers. To shop safely:

1. Start by identifying reputable retailers.
2. Look for well-known brands or store names you recognize. If you're exploring lesser-known sites, check for reviews and ratings from other customers, who can often

provide insight into the company's reliability and service quality.

3. Pay attention to the website's design as well; professional-looking sites with clear, error-free writing are more likely to be trustworthy.

Secure websites with URLs that start with **https://** indicate they are protected by SSL (Secure Socket Layer) encryption, making them safer for financial transactions. Red flags include:

- Deals that seem too good to be true
- Lack of clear contact information
- Sites asking for more personal information than necessary for making a purchase

<u>Making a Purchase</u>

Once you've found a reliable store, making a purchase should be straightforward but mindful. Start by carefully selecting your products. Read descriptions thoroughly to ensure the item meets your expectations, and check sizing charts when applicable. When ready, add items to your cart and proceed to checkout. Here, you'll enter your shipping information. Always double-check your address and contact details for accuracy to avoid delivery issues.

Next, it's payment time. Credit cards are typically the safest way to pay because they come with fraud protection. Some credit card companies even offer virtual credit card numbers that can be used for online purchases to keep your actual card number secure. After entering your payment details, review your order once more before confirming the purchase. Most stores will send a confirmation email summarizing your order, which you should save or print as a receipt.

Protecting Personal Information

Protecting your personal information extends beyond careful sharing. Strong, unique passwords for each online account are crucial; consider using a password manager to generate and store them securely. Always log out of shopping sites, especially when using shared or public computers. Ensuring your home Wi-Fi is secured with a robust password is equally important, as unsecured networks can be easy targets for hackers. Additionally, be cautious with the personal data you share. No shopping site needs your Social Security number or birthday to do business. The more they know, the more you are at risk if they suffer a data breach. Stay informed about the privacy policies of the places where you shop to understand how your information can be used and protected.

Handling Returns and Refunds

Even with careful shopping, you might need to return an item. Understanding the online store's return policy, even before you make a purchase, can save you a lot of headaches. Most policies are listed on the retailer's website, often in the footer under RETURNS or FAQ. Check if they offer free returns, require the items to be in original packaging, or if there are restocking fees.

To initiate a return, follow the instructions, which usually involve printing a return shipping label and packing the items securely. Keeping track of your return with shipping confirmations or tracking numbers is wise, as it helps ensure you receive your refund or exchange. Contact customer service for assistance if issues arise, such as delayed or denied refunds. Knowing your rights as a consumer can empower you to resolve such issues effectively.

Navigating the world of online shopping can be as rewarding as it is convenient, provided you take the necessary steps to shop safely.

By choosing reputable stores, making secure purchases, protecting your data, and understanding return policies, you can enjoy the benefits of shopping online with confidence and ease. Whether buying a new gadget to explore your tech-savvy side or ordering a book to unwind, remember that the digital marketplace is vast. With the proper knowledge, it's all within your safe reach.

1.5 USING APPS TO ENHANCE DAILY LIFE: HEALTH, READING, AND PRODUCTIVITY

Think of your smartphone as a Swiss Army knife for modern life; it's not just for calls or texts but a powerhouse tool for managing your health, enjoying literature and learning, and keeping your daily activities well organized. Let's explore how specific apps can transform your phone into your personal assistant, health coach, and mini-library.

<u>Health and Fitness Apps</u>

Maintaining a healthy lifestyle becomes increasingly important as we age, and thankfully, technology is here to make it easier. Health and fitness apps are like having a personal trainer and health monitor right in your pocket. For starters, apps like Fitbit or Apple Health track your daily steps and physical activities and monitor your heart rate and sleep patterns. Imagine going for a morning walk and having all the data about your heart rate and calories burned right at your fingertips, encouraging you each day to do a bit more, or perhaps just enough to keep you feeling great.

I have been using the app HIIT & Tabata for years, which allows me to set up my own High-Intensity Interval Training at home. I couldn't do without it anymore.

Then, there are medication reminder apps like Medisafe, which are invaluable for managing multiple medications. They not only remind you to take your pills but can also warn you about potential drug interactions and side effects. It's like having a pharmacist on call, ensuring your daily safety and well-being. These apps often include features to share information with your doctor or family members, so if you ever feel overwhelmed, help is just a few taps away. This kind of technology empowers you to take charge of your health, giving you the clarity and control needed to maintain your wellness simply and independently.

Reading and Learning Apps

The joy of losing yourself in a good book or discovering new knowledge doesn't diminish with age. Apps like Kindle and Audible have revolutionized how we consume literature and learning materials. With Kindle, your entire library can be in your hand, saving you the trip to the bookstore or library, not to mention the space physical books occupy. The app also allows you to adjust the font size and background colour, making reading as easy on the eyes as possible. Audible, on the other hand, brings books to life through audio. Whether you're resting your eyes or keeping your hands busy with gardening, you can continue 'reading' your favourite novels or learning about new subjects.

For those hungry for knowledge, platforms like Coursera or Khan Academy offer courses on everything from photography to philosophy. These apps provide access to lectures from top universities and learning institutions worldwide, often free or at a minimal cost. It's like going back to college without the pressure of grades or deadlines, learning purely for the joy and enrichment of it. You can explore short courses or dive into more extensive programs, all designed to keep your mind sharp and engaged.

Productivity Tools

Managing time and tasks efficiently becomes crucial as we fill our days with activities we love. Productivity apps help streamline your daily routines, ensuring you spend less time organizing and more time enjoying. Calendar apps like Google Calendar or the Calendar on your iPhone can be your everyday planners. They allow you to keep track of appointments, birthdays, and events, sending you reminders so you never miss a beat.

Then there are note-taking apps like Evernote or Microsoft OneNote, where you can jot down everything from your grocery lists to ideas for your next big project. These apps sync across all your devices, ensuring you have your notes wherever you go.

Reminder apps are another benefit, helping you manage daily tasks with ease. Set a reminder to water the plants, call a friend, or even take a break and stretch—whatever keeps your day running smoothly. These tools are designed to reduce the mental load of remembering every little task, giving you peace of mind and freeing up your mental space for more enjoyable or creative pursuits.

Security Essentials

While these apps bring many benefits, securing them is the most important step. Security apps such as Avast or McAfee can protect your smartphone from viruses and malware, which are as harmful to your digital health as physical ailments are to your body. These security tools scan your apps and files, blocking any malicious software before it can cause harm. Just as you would lock your doors at night, consider these apps to add a secure lock to your digital presence.

Moreover, keeping your apps updated is crucial for security. Developers regularly update apps to patch vulnerabilities and enhance functionalities. Neglecting updates can leave you exposed to risks. Most smartphones offer automatic update options, ensuring you're always protected without lifting a finger. Think of it as a continuous health check-up for your apps, keeping them in top shape to serve you better.

As you integrate these tools into your daily life, you'll find they bring not only convenience and enjoyment but also a greater sense of control and engagement with the modern world. Apps are designed to make life easier, allowing you to focus more on living well and less on the logistics that come with it. Whether it's through staying healthy, enjoying books, learning new subjects, or managing your day-to-day tasks, your smartphone is there to support your lifestyle. So go ahead—explore these apps and tailor your digital device to be the perfect companion in your retirement adventure.

1.6 EXPLORING THE WORLD OF BLOGGING: START YOUR OWN BLOG

If you've ever felt that surge of excitement when sharing your stories or perspectives with friends, you might find a delightful outlet in blogging. Picture this: your very own corner on the internet where you can express yourself, share your wisdom, and connect with like-minded individuals across the globe. Whether you're passionate about gardening, your travels, or even your culinary experiments, blogging allows you to weave your narrative into the vast digital tapestry. Let's walk through the basics of starting your blog, from selecting the right platform to creating engaging content and growing your audience.

Choosing a Blogging Platform

The first step in starting a blog is choosing where to build it. Two of the most user-friendly platforms that cater wonderfully to beginners are WordPress and Blogger. Each has unique advantages and slight drawbacks, so your choice will depend on your needs.

WordPress is immensely popular due to its flexibility and many features. It offers countless themes and plugins that customize your blog to your heart's content. Whether you want a simple design or something more sophisticated, WordPress likely has a solution. However, this abundance of options can sometimes overwhelm new users who prefer simplicity.

Blogger, on the other hand, is known for its straightforwardness and ease of use, making it an excellent choice for those who want to focus purely on writing without fussing too much over design options. Owned by Google, it provides a stable and secure platform with less customization than WordPress but enough features to run a basic blog beautifully. The trade-off with Blogger is that while it's easier to use, it offers less potential for growth or customization than WordPress does if you later decide to expand your blogging journey.

Setting Up a Blog

Once you've chosen your platform, setting up your blog is the next exciting step. Begin by selecting a template that aligns with the vision of your blog. Both WordPress and Blogger offer a range of free templates that you can start with. These templates are like a magazine layout; they dictate how your blog will appear to visitors, so pick one that brings to life the overall feeling you're aiming for.

After choosing a template, it's time to customize it. Experiment with colors, fonts, and layout options until you feel they genuinely represent your style. Next, set up the basic pages: an ABOUT ME page where you introduce yourself and your blog's purpose, a CONTACT page, and of course, the BLOG section where your posts will live.

Writing your first post can feel daunting, but remember, your blog is your space to express yourself. Think about what you're passionate about or what valuable information you can share, and just start writing. Your first post could introduce who you are and what readers can expect from your blog, setting the stage for future posts.

Content Creation Tips

Creating compelling content consistently is critical to a successful blog. Start by brainstorming topics that you're passionate about. This passion will shine through your writing and engage your readers. Plan your posts around these topics in a content calendar, which helps you maintain a consistent posting schedule. Aim to post regularly, whether it's once a week or a few times a month, as this consistency helps build a loyal readership. Post only as often as will comfortably fit into your schedule without being over-whelming—there are no requirements for how often you have to post.

Engaging with your readers is also crucial. Encourage comments by ending your posts with a question or a call-to-action, such as asking readers for their opinions or experiences related to the post topic. Respond to comments to foster a community feeling and show your readers that you value their input.

Promoting the Blog

Once your blog is up and running, promoting it helps you reach a wider audience. Start by sharing your posts on social media platforms like Facebook, Instagram, or Pinterest. If you've already set up social media profiles, share your posts regularly and engage with your followers there. You can also join blogging communities or forums related to your blog's topics, where you can share your posts and connect with other bloggers.

Email newsletters are another effective promotional tool. Encourage your readers to subscribe to your newsletter and use it to notify them about new posts or special content. This direct line of communication keeps your readers engaged and coming back for more.

Lastly, connecting with other bloggers can provide mutual benefits. Guest posting on each other's blogs or simply promoting each other's content can help you reach a broader audience and build professional relationships within the blogging community.

Blogging can be profoundly rewarding, providing a platform to share your stories, insights, and creativity. As you begin this adventure, remember that every blogger started with a single post. Your unique voice and perspectives will make your blog resonate with others. So take the leap, start writing, and watch your blog grow into a thriving community of engaged readers who appreciate what you have to share.

CHAPTER 2: ACTIVE LIVING AND FITNESS

Welcome to a chapter that pulses with the rhythm of active living—your guide to embracing a physically engaging lifestyle even as you enjoy your post-work life. Imagine each day unfurling new opportunities to move and enhance your well-being, invigorate your spirit, and expand your capabilities.

I go to the beach every morning as soon as I wake up for a walk across the shore line; it's such a great way to start the day, feeling the sand and the water between your toes, seeing the sun rise and feeling all pumped up to enjoy a new day.

In this chapter,we explore activities that align gracefully with your pace and preferences, ensuring that fitness remains a joy, not a chore. Let's lace up those sneakers, roll out the yoga mats, and dive into the delightful world of active living and fitness, tailor-made for the vibrant retiree.

2.1 YOGA FOR EVERY BODY: ADAPTING POSES FOR COMFORT AND SAFETY

Understanding Different Yoga Styles

Yoga, an ancient practice rooted in over 5,000 years of history, has evolved into various styles, each offering unique benefits and experiences. Understanding these differences for seniors or those seeking gentle, low-impact exercises can help them select the most suitable style.

Hatha yoga is recommended for beginners due to its slower pace and emphasis on basic poses and relaxation. In a Hatha class, you'll spend more time in each pose, which aids in understanding your body's movements and aligning them correctly.

Vinyasa yoga, known for its fluid, movement-intensive sequences, might initially seem daunting. However, many instructors offer modified versions that are less intense and more accessible for seniors. This style emphasizes the synchronization of breath with movement, providing a therapeutic way to improve flexibility and heart health.

Restorative yoga is among the best options for those interested in a profoundly nurturing practice. It uses props like cushions, blankets, and yoga blocks to support the body in different poses, allowing you to hold poses longer with greater comfort. This style focuses on relaxation and stress reduction, making it ideal for seniors looking to reduce anxiety and improve sleep quality.

Each of these styles holds the potential to enrich your retirement by improving physical flexibility and mental clarity. When choosing a class, consider visiting a few different types to see which atmosphere and style resonate most with you. Many yoga studios offer trial sessions for beginners, providing a perfect opportunity to explore without commitment.

Adapting Yoga Poses

One of the great things about yoga is its adaptability. Almost any pose can be modified to fit your comfort level and physical capability. For instance, if a standard yoga pose requires more flexibility or balance than you currently have, using props can offer support and stability. A chair can be used for seated poses or as a balance aid for standing poses. Yoga blocks are handy for supporting your hands in poses where you can't reach the floor, reducing strain and risk of injury.

For example, the classic 'Tree Pose' improves balance, but standing on one leg can be challenging. By performing this pose next to a chair, you can hold onto the back for support as you gradually build your balancing skills. Similarly, the 'Warrior' pose, which helps strengthen your legs and improve focus, can be done using a wall for back support, ensuring safety while you perfect the stance.

When adapting poses, the key is to maintain the integrity of the pose while ensuring it is comfortable and safe for you. Never hesitate to use as many modifications as you need, and always move within a range of motion that feels good. Remember, the goal of yoga is not perfection but progress and personal comfort.

Safety First

As with any physical activity, safety in yoga is paramount, especially as our bodies age. Listening to your body is the most critical safety rule in yoga. If a pose causes pain or discomfort, ease up or try a modification. Yoga should never hurt. It's also wise to avoid overexertion, which can lead to injuries. Instead, focus on gradual improvement and always listen to what your body tells you.

Before starting any new exercise regimen, including yoga, it's advisable to consult with a healthcare provider, especially if you have existing health conditions or concerns. Additionally, seeking advice from a professional yoga instructor can provide valuable insights into which poses may be most beneficial and safe for you.

Benefits of Regular Practice

The benefits of regular yoga practice extend far beyond physical improvements. While it's well-known for enhancing flexibility and strengthening muscles, yoga also offers significant mental health benefits. Regular practice can improve stress management through deep breathing techniques and mindfulness exercises. Many practitioners also report improved mood and mental clarity, thanks to the meditative aspects of yoga.

Moreover, yoga can be particularly beneficial in improving posture and balance, decreasing the risk of falls—a common concern for many seniors. Integrating yoga into your weekly routine allows you to enjoy a comprehensive workout that keeps your body strong and promotes a peaceful, resilient mind.

Incorporating yoga into your life as a retiree opens up a refreshing path to wellness that respects your body's needs and challenges its capabilities in a nurturing way. Whether mastering a new pose or simply enjoying a moment of relaxation, yoga offers a versatile toolkit for anyone looking to enhance their golden years with health and happiness. So, why not give it a try? Roll out your mat, take a deep breath, and let the journey unfold.

2.2 WATER AEROBICS: A LOW-IMPACT EXERCISE FOR STRENGTH AND STAMINA

Water aerobics is not just a refreshing way to bring fitness into your life; it's also wonderfully forgiving on the joints and suitable for all fitness levels. If you're considering joining a water aerobics class, the first step is finding the right fit for your needs and preferences. Look for classes tailored for seniors or offering various intensity levels. Many community pools and fitness centers provide classes labeled as 'gentle' or 'low-impact'. They're designed for older adults or those just starting their fitness journey.

When checking out a new class, don't hesitate to ask about the instructor's qualifications, particularly their experience with senior fitness. An instructor who understands the nuances of training older adults will ensure exercises are performed safely and effectively, minimizing the risk of injury.

You might wonder what equipment you'll need when attending your first class. Typically, water aerobics classes use several tools to enhance the workout. Water dumbbells or water weights are typical; they're lighter than traditional weights but provide resistance due to the water, which strengthens your muscles as you push them through the water. Noodles—large foam cylinders—are often used for balance exercises or to increase resistance. As for what to wear, comfort and safety are key. Choose a well-fitting swimsuit, and consider water shoes to improve traction on the pool floor, reducing the risk of slipping.

Engaging in water aerobics offers numerous exercises to adapt to your comfort and fitness level. A basic yet effective exercise you might encounter is the aqua jog. In waist-high water, perform a jogging motion; the water's resistance will increase the effort you need to exert, effectively building your cardiovascular health and muscle strength without strain on your joints.

Another common exercise is the leg lift, where you use the side of the pool or a noodle for support as you lift each leg in front of you, to the side, and then behind. This exercise targets your leg and core muscles, enhancing strength and flexibility. The beauty of water aerobics lies in the water's buoyancy, which supports your body weight, making movements smoother and reducing the impact on your bones and joints.

Besides the physical benefits, water aerobics classes offer a vibrant social environment. Joining a class can connect you with like-minded individuals who are also on a journey to maintain their health and vitality. This social interaction is a fantastic way to combat loneliness and keep your spirits high, contributing to overall mental health.

Regularly attending classes boosts your physical health through cardiovascular and muscle-strengthening activities and keeps you connected to a community. Each session in the pool is an opportunity to share experiences, encourage one another, and build friendships, all while enjoying the numerous health benefits of water aerobics. So, why not take the plunge? It's a fun, safe, and social way to stay active, offering a refreshing twist to your fitness routine

2.3 WALKING CLUBS: HOW TO START ONE IN YOUR COMMUNITY

If you've ever enjoyed a leisurely stroll through your neighborhood or a brisk walk in the park and thought, "This would be even better with friends," then starting a walking club could be a fantastic venture for you. Imagine regular gatherings where laughter and conversations flow as freely as your steps. Setting up a walking club in your community promotes physical activity and strengthens social ties, making each walk something to look forward to. Here's how to start organizing a walking club that keeps everyone eager to lace up their sneakers.

First, gauge interest. You might start with a few neighbors or friends who share your enthusiasm for walking. Extend an invitation to join your walking club via community bulletin boards, social media groups, or local newsletters. Be clear about what your club entails and what potential members might gain from joining. Once you have a group of interested individuals, decide collectively on how often you would like to meet—daily, a few times a week, or weekly—and the best time of day for everyone involved. Consistency is vital to building a habit and fostering group cohesion.

Next, consider the various routes you could take. It's a good idea to have multiple options to maintain interest. Routes can vary in scenery, difficulty, and length. Some days, you might explore a local park, while other times, you could walk through different neighborhoods or along a waterfront. Ensure the routes are safe and accessible for all members, considering factors like traffic, the condition of sidewalks or pathways, and the availability of rest areas, especially important for longer walks.

Setting up an effective communication channel is crucial. This could be an email list, a WhatsApp group, or a Facebook group where members can receive updates about meeting times and locations, share photos or interesting sights from their walks, and discuss ideas or feedback about the club. This keeps everyone informed and engaged, even when not physically together.

Walking safely should always be a priority, especially when dealing with varying weather conditions and environments. Encourage members to wear appropriate footwear—shoes that offer good support and are suitable for walking distances. Discuss the importance of dressing in layers to adjust comfortably to changes in weather and stress the necessity of bringing water, sunscreen, or hats on sunny days. Reminding everyone about the importance of good walking posture to avoid strain is also beneficial: keeping the head up, shoulders relaxed, and back straight.

Incorporating social elements can greatly enhance the walking club experience. Themed walks are a delightful way to keep the interest high. For instance, a nature walk during the fall can involve leaf-peeping and bird-watching, while a spring walk might focus on wildflower sightings. Photo walks encourage members to bring their cameras or use their smartphones to capture moments of beauty along the route, sparking creativity and offering a different focus. Seasonal walks, like a haunted history walk near Halloween or a holiday lights walk in December, add a festive element. Another enriching option is to include local history tours where members can learn about historical landmarks or significant events in the community during their walk.

Lastly, tracking progress can be both motivating and rewarding. Tools and apps like AllTrails are fantastic for planning routes and tracking your walks. These apps often provide detailed maps, user reviews, and the ability to track your distance and time. I have been using AllTrails for years, and finding new trails in any new location is fantastic. You can download the trail map upfront to walk without issues if you don't have cellular coverage.

Encouraging members to set personal goals or group challenges, such as total steps taken or collective miles walked over a month, can turn walking into a fun and fulfilling experience. Celebrating these achievements during your meetings can boost morale and improve the sense of community within the club.

Setting up and running a walking club can be a simple yet deeply rewarding way to connect with others and stay active. With each step, you improve your physical health and weave a richer, more connected community. So, why wait? Gather your friends, plan your routes, and step into the simple joy of walking together.

2.4 TAI CHI FOR BALANCE AND MENTAL CLARITY

Tai Chi, often referred to as meditation in motion, is more than just an exercise—it's a graceful form of art that helps connect the body and mind through gentle and flowing movements. Originating from ancient China, Tai Chi is rooted in martial arts, and over centuries, it has evolved into a practice that offers numerous health benefits, especially suited for the pace and needs of retirees.

The essence of Tai Chi lies in its slow, deliberate movements and controlled breathing, which together foster physical balance and mental tranquility. This unique blend of movement and meditation not only helps improve physical flexibility and balance but also calms the mind, encouraging a state of relaxation and clarity.

For those new to Tai Chi, understanding its fundamental principles is the first step toward integrating this practice into your life. Tai Chi movements are designed to flow smoothly from one to another, guided by a principle called 'jing,' which means calmness or balance. Jing is achieved through consistent practice that focuses on precision and fluidity. Each posture flows into the next without pause, ensuring your body is in constant motion. With names like 'Wave Hands like Clouds' and 'Grasp the Sparrow's Tail,' the poetic nature of the movements contributes to the mental image and understanding of the technique, making the physical execution an artistic expression and a health practice.

Learning Tai Chi can start in the comfort of your home or a more structured class setting. It's often beneficial for beginners to start with a class where a qualified instructor can guide you through the movements and ensure you perform them correctly. Basic movements in Tai Chi include hand motions, such as palm rotations, which help develop your dexterity and hand-eye coordination.

Stance work, such as the "horse stance", which involves standing with your feet wide apart and knees slightly bent, helps strengthen your legs and improve balance. The beauty of these exercises is that they can be adapted to any fitness level and can be made more challenging as your balance and strength improve.

The benefits of Tai Chi for seniors are particularly significant. Regular practice can improve balance, which is crucial in reducing the risk of falls, a common concern among older adults. The slow, controlled movements strengthen muscles and joints, enhancing physical stability. Moreover, focusing on deep breathing and mindfulness can significantly reduce stress and anxiety, creating a sense of well-being and relaxation. Many practitioners also report improvements in overall mood and sleep patterns, further contributing to an enhanced quality of life.

Finding the right Tai Chi instructor is crucial to ensure you gain the most from your practice. When searching for a class, look for an instructor experienced in teaching Tai Chi to beginners and who understands the physical limitations that may come with age.

A good instructor will teach you the movements, explain their purpose, and help you understand the flow and rhythm that characterize Tai Chi practice. They should be patient, attentive, and willing to adapt exercises to meet individual needs. Classes designed specifically for seniors or those emphasizing gentle Tai Chi are often the best options.

Incorporating Tai Chi into your routine can be a rewarding experience that enhances your physical health and mental clarity. Whether practiced in a serene park in the early morning or a quiet corner of your living room, Tai Chi offers a peaceful retreat from the hustle and bustle of daily life, inviting you to slow down and connect deeply with yourself. As you continue to practice, the balance you develop on the mat extends into other areas of your life, bringing with it a profound sense of calm and resilience that enhances your overall well-being.

So why not take the first step and explore the gentle yet powerful world of Tai Chi? The benefits can be truly transformative, offering a path to a healthier, more balanced life as you navigate the adventures of retirement.

2.5 SIMPLE HOME EXERCISES TO MAINTAIN MUSCLE HEALTH

Staying active and maintaining muscle health doesn't always require a gym membership or fancy equipment. You can achieve a full-body workout right in the comfort of your home using your body weight and everyday household items. Let's explore some essential exercises that are perfect for keeping you strong and agile and that you can easily integrate into your daily routine. If you like, you can find countless YouTube videos with exercises like these. Seated leg lifts, wall push-ups, and chair squats are excellent starters.

Seated leg lifts are fantastic for **strengthening your thigh and abdominal muscles** without putting stress on your back. Sit on a sturdy chair, extend one leg out straight, hold for a few seconds, and then raise it as high as comfortable. Alternate legs and try to do ten lifts per leg. You can do this exercise while watching TV or reading a book.

Wall push-ups are an excellent alternative to traditional floor push-ups, reducing strain on your wrists and back. Stand an arm's length from a wall, place your palms on the wall at shoulder height and width, then bend your elbows to bring your chest to the wall before pushing back to the starting position. This exercise **strengthens your chest, shoulders, and arms**.

Chair squats **strengthen your thighs, hips, and buttocks**. Start by sitting in a chair. Stand up to a complete stand without leaning forward too much, then slowly sit back down and repeat.

Creating a routine that fits into your life is crucial for consistency, which is critical to seeing results. Consider your daily schedule and how you can incorporate a short exercise session. Ten minutes of leg lifts and push-ups after breakfast, followed by another ten minutes of chair squats and stretches in the afternoon. Of course, this is only an example, and doing anything more than you are currently doing is a plus.

To help you stay on track, think about creating a simple chart or using an app to log your activities. Some retirees find it helpful to have visual reminders, such as a printed schedule on the fridge or a digital prompt on their phone. If you're tech-savvy, scanning a QR code to access a pre-planned weekly exercise routine online can be a convenient way to keep your regimen fresh and exciting.

Using household items as improvised gym equipment is a clever way to enhance your workout without buying weights or machines. Filled water bottles make excellent dumbbells for arm curls or can add extra resistance to your leg lifts—canned goods can also serve the same purpose. A bag of rice or a laundry detergent bottle can be effective if you need something heavier. You can also use towels, scarves, or belts as resistance bands for stretching exercises or to add an element of stability training to your workouts.

The benefits of regular exercise are immense. Engaging in a daily routine helps maintain muscle mass, which naturally declines with age. Strong muscles are crucial for everyday activities like carrying groceries or climbing stairs and play a vital role in managing your weight and boosting your metabolism. Exercise also improves mobility and balance, which can help prevent falls. Moreover, daily exercise can bring structure to your day, boost your mood, and increase your overall independence, allowing you to enjoy a more active and fulfilling lifestyle.

Embracing these simple exercises as part of your daily routine can significantly enhance your quality of life. They provide a practical and enjoyable way to strengthen your body, improve your health, and maintain your independence. So, consider how you can integrate these activities into your day and start enjoying the benefits of an active and healthy lifestyle right in your own home.

2.6 CYCLING FOR FUN: CHOOSING THE RIGHT BIKE FOR SENIORS

Cycling is a wonderful way to enjoy the outdoors, improve your health, and even meet new friends. But as we age, the features we need in a bicycle can change. Finding the right bike can help maintain your cycling joy and ensure your comfort and safety. Certain types of bicycles, such as those with step-through frames, three-wheelers, and electric bikes, can be particularly advantageous for seniors.

Step-through frames are ideal because they don't require you to lift your leg high to get on the bike, which makes mounting and dismounting much easier and safer. This frame type is very accommodating if you have limited flexibility or balance. Three-wheelers, or trikes, offer enhanced stability; you don't have to balance them at all, which can be a relief if you find maintaining balance challenging or are carrying groceries or other loads. Electric bikes, or e-bikes, come equipped with a battery-powered "assist" that comes via pedaling and, in some models, a throttle. They can be perfect if you enjoy longer rides but may need more stamina than you once had, as the electric assist can help you conquer hills and cover greater distances with less fatigue.

Regarding safety gear, wearing a helmet is non-negotiable, regardless of age or experience level. Helmets significantly reduce the risk of head injuries in the event of a fall. Make sure your helmet fits well; it should sit level on your head and snugly beneath your chin. Reflective clothing is also essential, especially if you enjoy riding in the early morning or late evening. Select bright colors and reflective materials that make you visible to drivers. Gloves can improve grip and protect your hands in a fall, while padded shorts can increase comfort during longer rides.

Maintaining your bike is crucial to ensure it remains safe to use. Regular maintenance checks, either done by yourself or a professional, should include checking tire pressure, brakes, and chain lubrication. Maintenance ensures your bike is safe and can extend its lifespan and enhance performance.

Planning Safe Routes

Selecting suitable cycling routes is vital, especially to avoid heavy traffic and areas with poor road conditions. Start by identifying bike lanes and trails in your area, which are typically safer than riding on the road.

I grew up in the Netherlands, probably the most biker-friendly country in the world. There are bike lanes everywhere.

Many cities have maps of bike-friendly roads and paths, often found at local bike shops or city websites. Look for routes that are flat and have rest areas, especially if you are just getting back into cycling or prefer a leisurely pace. These rest stops are great for taking a break, enjoying the scenery, and staying hydrated.

Apps and GPS devices can be incredibly helpful in planning and navigating your routes. Some apps provide detailed information about the terrain, traffic levels, and even the availability of bike lanes. They can also help you track your distance and find the easiest route to your destination, making your ride smoother and more enjoyable.

Community Cycling Groups

Joining a cycling group can significantly enhance the social enjoyment of cycling. These groups often organize regular rides, providing a fantastic opportunity to meet people, explore new areas, and share cycling tips and stories. Look for groups or clubs in your community that cater to seniors or offer rides for all skill levels. This provides social interaction and adds a layer of safety as you ride with others who can help with a mechanical problem or emergency.

Many community centers and bike shops offer group rides and cycling clinics for seniors. These can be a great way to learn more about cycling and meet other cyclists who share your enthusiasm for the sport. Some cities even host senior-specific cycling events, such as races or leisure rides, which can add a fun and competitive element to your cycling experience.

Cycling is more than just physical exercise; it's a way to enjoy freedom, fresh air, and camaraderie. With the right bike, safety measures, well-chosen routes, and community involvement, cycling can continue to be a joyful, rewarding activity well into retirement. It keeps you physically active and engages you socially and mentally, enriching your life in numerous ways.

As we wrap up this chapter on Active Living and Fitness, remember that every activity discussed here is more than just a way to stay fit. Whether it's yoga, water aerobics, walking, Tai Chi, or cycling, each offers unique benefits that can enhance your physical health, mental well-being, and social life. Each step, pedal, or stretch is an investment in your quality of life. So, choose activities that resonate most with you, and let them inspire and energize your daily routine. As we turn the page, we'll explore new ways to enhance our lives through travel and adventure, promising new experiences and unforgettable memories.

CHAPTER 3: TRAVEL AND EXPLORATION

Imagine rolling down scenic highways with the windows down, your favorite tunes playing, and a landscape that changes with every mile you cover. Road trips are not just about reaching a destination; they're about rediscovering the joy of the journey itself, the freedom of the open road, and the excitement of exploring new places at your own pace.

As a retiree, you have the luxury of time, making road trips a perfect way to explore without the rush, allowing you to soak in every experience. In this chapter, we'll dive into how you can plan a budget-friendly road trip that's as enjoyable as it is economical. From selecting the right vehicle to mapping out your journey and packing the essentials, get ready to steer your way into an adventure tailored just for you.

3.1 PLANNING A BUDGET-FRIENDLY ROAD TRIP

Budgeting for a Road Trip

Effective budgeting is vital to enjoying a stress-free road trip. Start by estimating the main expenses: fuel, accommodation, food, and any attractions you may want to visit. To save on gas, consider traveling during off-peak hours to avoid heavy traffic, which consumes more fuel. There are apps available to help you find the cheapest gas stations along your route. Consider accommodations beyond hotels; vacation rentals, hostels, or even camping can offer more budget-friendly options. When it comes to meals, packing a cooler with snacks and sandwiches can reduce the need to eat out frequently, saving you a significant amount on food expenses. Also, many restaurants offer early-bird specials or senior discounts, so take advantage of those when you dine out.

Choosing the Right Vehicle

The vehicle type can make a significant difference in your road trip experience. Comfort and reliability are paramount, especially on longer drives. If your current vehicle isn't up to the task, renting a car could be a wise option—rental cars are typically newer, well-maintained, and more reliable for long distances. Moreover, renting a car can be economical in the long run by avoiding wear and tear on your own vehicle. When selecting a rental, consider models known for their comfort and fuel effi-ciency. Vehicles with features like good lumbar support, easy entry and exit, and modern safety features can enhance your driving experience, making your journey as comfortable as possible.

Mapping Out the Journey

The route you choose can define your road trip experience. With the help of travel apps and GPS, planning your journey has never been easier. Apps like Roadtrippers or Google Maps allow you to map your route while highlighting interesting stops and attrac-tions along the way. When planning, look for scenic roads that may take longer but are visually more rewarding and likely less crowded. Also, consider your comfort and driving preferences—plan for regular breaks every couple of hours to stretch your legs and perhaps a scenic spot for a picnic lunch. Check accessibility information if needed, ensuring that the stops along your journey are senior-friendly with easy access and good facilities.

Finally, consider the time of year for your trip with respect to climate and weather events that can occur in the area.

Packing Essentials

Packing wisely can help you avoid delays and complications while maximizing convenience and focus on enjoyment. Essentials include medications, comfortable clothing, and emergency contact information. It's also a good idea to bring a first aid kit, a road atlas in case of lost signal or GPS failure, and a spare mobile phone charger. Pack a flashlight, extra batteries, and essential car repair tools like a tire pressure gauge and jumper cables. For entertain-ment and comfort, consider audiobooks, travel pillows, and blan-kets, especially if you're sharing driving duties and have the chance to rest while someone else is at the wheel.

Traveling by road offers a unique kind of freedom—a chance to explore at your own pace, make spontaneous decisions, and create lasting memories. Whether it's marveling at a sunset from a highway overlook, discovering a charming small town, or enjoying a meal at a roadside diner, road trips provide a canvas for adventures that are as rich and varied as the landscapes you drive through. So buckle up and prepare for a journey that promises relaxation, discovery, and a renewed sense of adventure in the golden years of retirement.

3.2 VOLUNTOURISM OPPORTUNITIES FOR RETIREES

Voluntourism, a blend of volunteering and tourism, offers a unique opportunity to enrich your travel experiences by contributing to the communities you visit. It's about more than seeing new places; it's about engaging deeply with them and leaving a positive mark. For many retirees, voluntourism provides a sense of purpose and the chance to use their skills and experience meaningfully. Whether it's teaching English, assisting in wildlife conservation efforts, or helping build community facilities, these activities allow you to connect with local cultures and people on a level that typical tourism rarely touches. The beauty of voluntourism lies in its mutual benefit. While you bring valuable assistance to projects and communities, you gain an immersive experience that goes beyond the surface of conventional sightseeing.

Choosing the right voluntourism program makes all the difference. It starts with identifying what you're passionate about and what skills you can offer. Once you have a clear idea, research organizations that facilitate these opportunities. Look for well-established programs with a strong ethical practice and community involvement track record.

Reputable organizations should offer transparency about where your efforts and any donations are going. They should also prioritize the welfare and development of the local community and environment over the needs of volunteers. Checking reviews and testimonials from previous volunteers can provide insights into their experiences and the organization's on-ground impact. It's also wise to reach out directly to the organizers with any questions about the program's goals, the specific contributions you will be making, and the support you can expect while on location.

Preparation is key to a fulfilling voluntourism experience. Depending on your destination, you may need specific vaccinations or medical preparations several weeks before departure. Consult a travel doctor to ensure you have all the necessary health protections.

Travel insurance is another essential, covering everything from medical emergencies to trip cancellations. Delve into your destination's cultural norms and etiquette to ensure respectful interactions. Many organizations provide pre-trip training or resources to help you understand community expectations and the social landscape of the area. This can include basic language training, which helps in day-to-day interactions and deepens your connection with the community.

Documenting and sharing your voluntourism experiences can inspire others and spread the word about the causes you support. Consider keeping a blog or a social media diary of your journey, detailing the projects you work on, the challenges you encounter, and the successes you celebrate. Photos and stories can capture the impact of your work and the beauty of cross-cultural exchanges, offering a window into the world of voluntourism. These narratives can be powerful tools for raising awareness and encouraging others to engage in similar work, expanding the ripple effect of your efforts.

Voluntourism opens up a world where travel meets purpose, where each destination offers a chance to make a difference. For retirees, it's an incredibly enriching way to apply a lifetime of skills and experience in new, impactful ways. As you immerse yourself in different cultures, work alongside locals, and contribute to sustainable projects, you not only enhance your own life but also bring about positive change in the world. If you're looking for more than just a getaway and want to engage deeply with your travel destinations, voluntourism is the perfect path to fulfilling your adventurous and charitable spirit.

3.3 EXPLORING NATIONAL PARKS WITH SENIOR DISCOUNTS

The allure of national parks is undeniable. With sprawling landscapes, abundant wildlife, and the tranquility of nature, these parks offer a perfect escape into the beauty of the natural world. As a retiree, you can enjoy these magnificent places with the added benefit of senior discounts, making it both an economical and enriching experience. Many national parks across the globe offer discounted or even free entry, lodging, and tour options for seniors. In the United States, for instance, the America the Beautiful - National Parks and Federal Recreational Lands Senior Pass provides lifetime access to over 2,000 federal recreation sites for a one-time fee. Similar incentives are available in other countries, encouraging seniors to explore the natural beauty around them without straining their budgets.

Obtaining a senior pass is typically straightforward. In the U.S., you can apply for the pass online or in person at any federal recreation site that charges an entrance fee. The process involves verifying your age, usually requiring nothing more than a government-issued ID. The pass reduces costs and includes additional discounts on amenities like camping, swimming, boat launching, and guided tours, making it an invaluable resource for any nature-loving retiree. Each country has its application process that you might be familiar with already.

When selecting national parks, consider those known for their accessibility and senior-friendly facilities. Parks with well-maintained trails, clear signage, ample rest areas, and robust visitor centers offer a more comfortable and enjoyable experience. For example, Yosemite National Park in the U.S. provides accessible shuttle buses, wheelchair-friendly viewpoints, and a range of lodging options that cater to different mobility needs. Internationally, places like the Peak District in the UK, Plitvice Lakes National Park in Croatia, and Banff National Park in Canada offer similar conveniences, ensuring their natural splendors are accessible to everyone.

Exploring these parks, you'll find no shortage of activities perfectly suited to senior adventurers. Bird watching is a popular and relaxing way to connect with nature. Many parks offer guided bird-watching tours, or you can venture out with a field guide and binoculars. Photography is another excellent way to engage with the environment. The diverse landscapes—from towering forests and serene lakes to majestic mountains—provide endless opportunities to capture stunning images. For those who enjoy more activity, consider short hikes on marked and maintained trails. These hikes are often designed with less elevation and rugged terrain, making them manageable and enjoyable. Always check the park's visitor center for maps and advice on trails that match your comfort level.

Safety is paramount when enjoying the outdoors. Always keep an eye on the weather conditions, as weather in national parks can change rapidly. Dress in layers so you can adjust to temperature fluctuations throughout the day. Staying hydrated is crucial, especially in warmer climates or during more strenuous activities, so carry enough water. Be aware of the wildlife in the area. At the same time, encounters are often a highlight, and maintaining a safe distance ensures both your safety and the well-being of the animals. It's wise to carry a basic first aid kit for minor injuries and always let someone know your plans, especially if venturing out alone.

By taking advantage of senior discounts and choosing suitable parks and activities, you can enjoy the immense benefits of spending time in nature. Whether it's the tranquility of a quiet forest, the thrill of spotting rare wildlife, or the satisfaction of capturing a perfect sunrise on your camera, national parks offer many experiences that can enrich your retirement years. So pack your essentials, grab your pass, and immerse yourself in the natural beauty that awaits in these national and international treasures.

3.4 SAFE AND ENGAGING SOLO TRAVEL DESTINATIONS

Embarking on solo travel can be one of life's most valuable experiences, particularly when you have the freedom that retirement affords. Choosing destinations that are not only safe but also known for their hospitality and accessibility can significantly enhance your travel experience. Places like New Zealand, Portugal, and Japan are top for solo senior travelers due to their low crime rates, friendly locals, and well-organized transport systems.

New Zealand's stunning landscapes are matched by its commitment to safety and a well-structured tourism sector that makes navigating the beautiful islands straightforward and stress-free. Portugal offers a warm Southern European welcome with easy-to-navigate cities like Lisbon and Porto, compact and packed with culture and history. Japan is renowned for its impeccable safety standards and the politeness of its people, alongside an efficient public transportation system that makes traveling alone a breeze.

Solo travel opens up a unique avenue for personal growth and freedom. It allows you to explore new environments at your own pace, make decisions based on your interests, and step out of your comfort zone, leading to increased self-confidence and independence. The thrill of discovering a new city on your terms, deciding spontaneously to visit a museum or sit in a café and people-watch, can be incredibly liberating. It's also a fantastic opportunity to meet new people, whether they are locals or fellow travelers. Engaging with different cultures and forming new friendships can enrich your travel experience and provide insights into the world that you might not encounter in any other way.

Staying connected with family and friends back home is important, especially when traveling alone. Technology makes this easier than ever. Before you leave, make sure your mobile device is set up with international capabilities, or consider purchasing a local SIM card upon arrival for access to data and local calls. Apps like WhatsApp, Skype, and FaceTime allow you to keep in touch with loved ones via text, voice calls, or video chats, ensuring you never feel disconnected from those you care about. Additionally, sharing your travel itinerary with family or a close friend is wise—they should know where you plan to be and when you're expected to check in.

Regarding health and safety, a few precautions can ensure your trip remains enjoyable and worry-free. Always purchase comprehensive travel insurance that covers health emergencies, trip cancellations, and baggage loss. Since unexpected health issues can arise, this becomes even more crucial as we age. Keep a list of emergency contacts on you, including the local emergency numbers for the countries you're visiting and contact information for your country's embassy or consulate.

Be aware of common scams targeting tourists; a little research before you go can alert you to what to watch out for. Always trust your instincts—steer clear if something doesn't feel right. Lastly, pack a basic first-aid kit with essentials like band-aids, pain relievers, and any prescription medications you need. Make sure your medications are clearly labeled, and consider carrying a doctor's note describing why you need them. This can be helpful at airport security or if you need to visit a local doctor.

Solo travel as a retiree offers a splendid tapestry of experiences, each destination holding the potential for new adventures and stories to tell. With the right preparation and a spirit of adventure, you can ensure these journeys are safe, smooth, and deeply rewarding. Whether wandering through ancient ruins, attending a lively city festival, or simply soaking in the natural beauty of a quiet beach, the world is yours to explore at your own pace, with each experience adding to your rich tapestry of memories.

3.5 CULTURAL TOURS DESIGNED FOR SENIORS

When planning your next travel adventure, consider a cultural tour tailored to seniors. These tours are designed with your comfort in mind, ensuring you can enjoy immersive cultural experiences without the hassle of planning every detail yourself. Selecting the right tour involves looking for options that balance engaging activities with ample downtime, offer accessible transportation, and provide clear information about the tour's physical demands.

Many companies now specialize in senior travel and understand the nuances of crafting fulfilling and manageable itineraries. Look for tours with a track record of positive reviews from senior travelers, and don't hesitate to contact the tour operators to ask about the pace of the tour and the level of physical activity involved. They should be able to provide detailed itineraries that include cultural sites, leisure time, and options for those who may want a slower pace.

The advantages of guided tours are numerous, especially for those who find travel logistics daunting. With expert tour guides, you gain deeper insights into the destinations' histories and cultures and enjoy the peace of mind of having all accommodations and transport pre-arranged. This can significantly reduce stress, allowing you to focus more on the experience rather than the details of travel planning.

Professional guides often have extensive local knowledge and can provide access to experiences you might not discover on your own. Moreover, they can adapt the tour in real-time to accommodate the group's interests and energy levels, ensuring every member has an enjoyable experience. Additionally, these tours often include meals, which means you'll have the opportunity to taste local cuisine in recommended restaurants, enhancing your cultural experience.

Interacting with local cultures is a highlight of any travel journey. Tour guides can facilitate meaningful exchanges that respect local traditions and customs. This might include arranging visits to local artisans, attending cultural performances, or even participating in workshops where you can learn a local craft or cooking style. These interactions enrich your travel experience, help support local economies, and preserve cultural heritage. It's essential to approach these activities openly and respectfully, embracing cultural differences and similarities. Guides can provide valuable context and help bridge the cultural gap, ensuring you and the locals have a positive and respectful exchange.

Learning about the destination's culture and history before you go is beneficial. Many cultural tours offer pre-trip reading lists or resources that can provide a foundational understanding of the places you'll visit. This preparation might include books, documentaries, or even a list of relevant websites and articles. Investing some time in these resources can deepen your appreciation of the sites you'll visit and enrich your interactions with locals. It can also spark curiosity and lead to more insightful questions and discussions during the tour. Learning a few phrases in the local language is also helpful in practical situations. It shows respect for the people you meet, often leading to warmer communication and a deeper connection to the community.

By choosing a cultural tour that caters to your needs as a senior, you're setting the stage for a travel experience that is as pleasurable as it is comfortable. You'll return home with more than just photos; you'll have stories of personal connections, deeper insights, and memorable encounters that only such immersive experiences can provide. So take the time to select a tour that resonates with your interests and physical comfort, and prepare to explore the world's variety of culture and history in the company of fellow travelers who share your sense of adventure and curiosity.

3.6 CRUISING 101: PICKING THE RIGHT CRUISE FOR SENIORS

Cruising offers a splendid blend of relaxation, adventure, and luxury, making it a favorite travel mode for many retirees. When it comes to choosing the right cruise line, think of it much like picking a new restaurant to try—it's all about matching your taste and comfort. Some cruise lines cater specifically to a more mature audience, offering a serene environment, age-appropriate entertainment, and itineraries that are appealing to seasoned travelers. These cruises often provide amenities such as ballroom dancing, classical music performances, and lectures on topics ranging from history to local cultures, ensuring that you have engaging activities that resonate with your interests.

Moreover, when selecting a cruise, consider the size and style of the ship. Smaller ships offer a more intimate and refined experience but may carry a higher price tag. Larger ships boast a vast array of amenities like multiple dining venues, spas, and even indoor pools. However, the size might be overwhelming, and the bustling atmosphere might not suit everyone's taste.

It's also worth considering the destinations the cruise line offers. Whether you dream of gliding through the fjords of Norway or basking in the sun on a Caribbean island, ensure the itinerary aligns with your travel aspirations. Many cruise lines also offer themed cruises, such as culinary or history-focused, which can heighten your experience by aligning with your interests.

Taking care of your health while on a cruise is crucial, especially as a retiree. Most modern cruise ships are well-equipped with medical facilities that can handle everything from minor ailments to more serious medical conditions. However, checking with the cruise line about the specific medical services available on board is advised before you book. If you have specific health needs, inquire whether the ship's medical center can cater to them. Additionally, it's essential to carry enough of any prescribed medications for the entire trip, as well as copies of your prescriptions and a note from your doctor detailing your medical conditions and necessary medications. This preparation ensures smooth sailing even if unexpected health issues arise.

Travel insurance is particularly important when cruising, as it can cover a range of potential inconveniences and emergencies, from trip cancellations to medical situations. Be sure to choose a policy that covers evacuations, as medical evacuations from a ship can be very expensive. Review the insurance policy carefully to ensure it covers the regions you will be visiting and any potential activities you plan to partake in during port calls.

Speaking of port calls, they are often highlights of a cruise, offering opportunities to explore new places and cultures. Planning is wise to make the most of these excursions. Research the ports you will visit and consider booking guided tours, especially in locations where language barriers or challenging terrain could make independent exploration difficult. Many cruise lines offer a range of shore excursions that cater to various activity levels, ensuring you can choose an experience that matches your physical capabilities and interests. For a more personalized experience, consider smaller, private tours offering more tailored and intimate exploration.

When exploring on your own, it's important to keep safety in mind. Stick to well-traveled areas and be aware of the local customs and laws. Wear comfortable walking shoes, carry water, and remember to take your ship's contact information with you in case you need assistance getting back. Also, ensure you leave enough time to return to the ship before departure, as the ship will not wait for late passengers.

Cruising as a retiree offers a fantastic blend of comfort, adventure, and the chance to see the world without the hassle of constant packing and unpacking. Whether you're looking for cultural enrichment, relaxation, or a bit of adventure, there's a cruise out there that's perfect for you. With the right preparation, a cruise can provide a wonderful travel experience, combining the comforts of luxury accommodation with the excitement of exploring new destinations.

As we conclude this chapter on Travel and Exploration, remember that each travel mode and destination offers unique joys and challenges. Whether navigating the roads on a budget-friendly trip, making meaningful contributions through voluntourism, enjoying the serene beauty of national parks, embarking on solo adventures, or cruising the high seas, the key is to embrace the opportunities for growth, enjoyment, and relaxation. As you turn the page to the next chapter, keep your spirit of adventure alive, ready to explore more ways to enrich your retirement years with new experiences and learning opportunities.

CHAPTER 4: LIFELONG LEARNING AND PERSONAL GROWTH

R emember the thrill of your first day back at school after a long summer? The crisp new notebooks, a box of sharp pencils, and an air of endless possibilities? That excitement doesn't have to be a distant memory. In fact, it can be a refreshing part of your retirement. Lifelong learning isn't just about keeping your mind sharp; it also brings fulfilment through new experiences, meeting people who share your interests, and even stepping into new adventures. Whether it's delving into a subject you've always been passionate about or challenging yourself with something completely unknown, the world of learning is open to you in ways it has never been before.

4.1 COMMUNITY COLLEGE CLASSES FOR SENIORS

Exploring Available Courses

Your local community college can be a treasure trove of learning opportunities, particularly suited for the vibrant life of a retiree. Many institutions offer a wide range of courses, from art and history to science and technology, tailored to engage learners of all ages.

Start by visiting the college's website or the campus in person to explore the course catalog. Many colleges have advisors who are happy to help seniors find classes that match their interests and skill levels. Don't shy away from technology or more contemporary courses either; these can be incredibly rewarding and offer practical skills to enhance your daily life.

When selecting courses, consider those that lead to new skills or hobbies that you can continue at home, like photography, gardening, or culinary arts. These classes not only provide knowledge but also practical experience through hands-on learning, making the educational process both engaging and functional. Additionally, many community colleges offer "audit" options for seniors, allowing you to attend classes at a reduced rate without receiving credit. This option is perfect if you're more interested in the joy of learning rather than earning another degree.

Benefits of Lifelong Learning

The benefits of engaging in lifelong learning, especially in a structured environment like a community college, extend far beyond acquiring knowledge. Cognitive benefits include enhanced memory, problem-solving skills, and verbal proficiency. Moreover, being a part of a learning community can significantly boost your social interactions, provide a sense of belonging, and reduce feelings of isolation, which are common in retirement.

Classes also encourage a routine similar to a work environment but without the pressure of performance reviews or deadlines. This structure can bring a satisfying rhythm to your week, giving you something exciting to look forward to. The social interactions in class—from group projects to class discussions—offer friendship and exposure to diverse perspectives, enriching your understanding of the world.

Registration and Discounts

Registering for classes at a community college is typically a straightforward process. You can usually register online, in person, or over the phone. When registering, inquire about any discounts or scholarships available for seniors. Many colleges offer significant tuition reductions for older adults, and some even allow seniors to attend classes for free on a space-available basis. These opportunities make learning more accessible and affordable, ensuring that finances are not a barrier to your educational pursuits.

<u>Participating in Campus Life</u>

Beyond the classroom, community colleges often boast vibrant campuses inviting students to fully immerse themselves in the college experience. Participate in campus events, join clubs that align with your interests, or attend guest lectures and workshops. These activities are enjoyable and offer additional opportunities to meet people and engage with the community.

For instance, attending a campus art show or joining a gardening club can connect you with fellow enthusiasts and provide a platform for sharing ideas and experiences. These connections can be deeply fulfilling, offering companionship and a shared joy in discovery. Engaging in campus life can improve your educational experience, making learning a dynamic part of your everyday life.

As you continue to explore and engage in lifelong learning, remember that every class, every lesson, and every new friend is a step toward an even more fulfilling retirement. Let your curiosity lead the way as you discover new passions and revive old ones, building a retirement that is as educational as it is enjoyable.

4.2 ONLINE COURSES IN HISTORY, ART, AND SCIENCE

Imagine turning your living room into a classroom where history, art, and science come to life through your computer screen. This is the beauty of online learning platforms like Coursera, Udemy, and Khan Academy. These platforms offer countless courses taught by esteemed educators and professionals from around the globe. Whether you're looking to unravel the mysteries of ancient civilizations, appreciate the nuances of modern art, or understand the basics of computer science, these platforms have something to cater to your diverse interests.

Choosing the right course might seem daunting initially, but these platforms are designed to help you navigate the options effortlessly. Start by exploring categories that catch your interest on each platform.

Coursera often partners with universities and offers structured courses that can even lead to certification or degrees, making it ideal if you're looking for an in-depth study on a subject. Udemy provides a wide range of courses focusing on skill development, which can be perfect if you want to learn something new, like photography or web development. Meanwhile, Khan Academy offers free courses, ideal for brushing up on subjects like math or science, providing a comprehensive understanding at a pace that suits you.

The key to making the most of these platforms is selecting the right course and engaging with the material. Most online courses are designed to be interactive. Participate in forums where you can discuss course materials with fellow learners from around the world. This strengthens your understanding and connects you with a community of like-minded individuals, expanding your learning beyond the digital classroom. Many courses also include assignments or projects, which provide a hands-on experience; completing these helps consolidate your learning and apply your new knowledge in practical scenarios.

Setting a realistic learning pace is crucial to enjoying and succeeding online courses. Unlike traditional classroom settings, online learning offers the flexibility to study at your own pace, which can be a significant advantage. However, this flexibility also requires self-discipline. Start by setting achievable goals each week or month, depending on the course structure. If a course feels overwhelming, most platforms allow you to adjust deadlines for assignments or suggest taking the course over a longer period.

Remember, the goal is to enjoy the process of learning without feeling rushed or stressed.

The range of courses available is vast and varied. If you're intrigued by history, you might find courses on ancient Egyptian art, the evolution of European architecture, or the significant wars that shaped the modern world. Art enthusiasts might enjoy exploring digital photography, graphic design, or fashion design courses. For those inclined toward science, options range from introductory courses in biology and chemistry to more specialized subjects like neuroscience or environmental science. Each course is designed to cater to learners at different levels of expertise and commitment, ensuring there is always something new and exciting to learn.

As you delve into these online courses, you'll find that learning is about acquiring knowledge and bringing new experiences and perspectives to your life. Each lesson brings a chance to challenge yourself, explore beyond your comfort zone, and connect with fascinating subjects and people who share your passions. So, why not take the first step and sign up for a course today? The world of history, art, science, and more awaits you to unfold its wonders.

4.3 WORKSHOPS ON WRITING YOUR LIFE STORY

Have you ever considered that your life, with all its ups and downs, twists and turns, could fill the pages of a book that might inspire, teach, or entertain? Writing your life story isn't just a way to preserve memories; it's a profound journey into understanding yourself and sharing your unique experiences with others.

Finding workshops tailored to writing personal histories is a beautiful starting point. These workshops are often available through local community centers, libraries, and online platforms

CHAPTER 4: LIFELONG LEARNING AND PERSONAL GROW...   69

where seasoned writers and educators guide you through the process of capturing your life on paper. Local universities may also offer continuing education classes focused on memoir writing, which is worth exploring. For those who prefer a more flexible schedule, online workshops provide resources and peer interaction without leaving your home. Websites like Writers' Digest or Gotham Writers Workshop offer structured courses with feedback from writing professionals.

Organizing your life experiences into a compelling narrative might seem daunting. Still, with guidance from these workshops, you can learn how to weave your memories into a story that resonates. Start by outlining the key moments that have shaped you—those pivotal events that offer rich, emotional, and impactful revelations. These don't have to be monumental on a global scale; often, the personal victories, the quiet moments of clarity, or the difficult struggles truly touch readers.

Structuring your story can follow a chronological approach, which is straightforward and orderly, or you might find a thematic structure more engaging, grouping life events by themes or lessons learned. Workshops can help you explore different structures and decide which works best for narrating your unique story.

Now, let's talk about the nuts and bolts of writing. Crafting a narrative that captures interest involves more than just laying out the facts; it's about bringing your story to life with vivid descriptions, engaging dialogue, and a pace that keeps readers wanting to turn the page. Descriptive writing helps paint a picture of your experiences, allowing readers to see, hear, and feel the moments you describe.

Dialogue can be a powerful tool in memoirs, bringing out personalities and conveying real-life conversations that add authenticity and depth. Managing the pace of your narrative is crucial too. Just like in a novel, the flow of events needs to maintain momentum. Balancing moments of tension with resolution keeps readers engaged and mirrors the natural rhythm of life's highs and lows. Workshops provide practical exercises in these areas, often allowing you to experiment and receive constructive feedback that hones your writing skills.

Finally, publishing your life story opens a new chapter where you share your insight and experience with a broader audience. Today's technology offers a variety of publishing options. Blogs and websites are excellent platforms for serializing your story, offering a space to share chapters as they are written and receiving immediate feedback from readers. For those who dream of seeing their work in print, self-publishing platforms like Amazon's Kindle Direct Publishing allow you to publish your life story as an ebook or a printed book without the need for traditional publishers.

Alternatively, if you prefer a more personal touch, creating hand-crafted booklets for family and friends can be a meaningful way to share your journey. Workshops often discuss these options, providing insights into the pros and cons of each and helping you navigate the path to publishing that best suits your aspirations.

Writing your life story is more than a mere recount of events—it's a process of reflection and celebration of the life you've lived. It's about telling your truth, learning from reflection, and leaving a legacy that inspires others. Whether shared publicly or kept within the family, the pages you create will be a testament to a life fully lived, filled with lessons, love, and legacy. So why not pick up a pen or open a laptop and start writing? The first word you write is the first step on the path to sharing your story with the world.

4.4 PHOTOGRAPHY CLASSES: CAPTURING LIFE'S MOMENTS

Photography, a hobby that can beautifully bridge the gap between technology and art, offers a rewarding way to capture and share the world as you see it. Whether you're drawn to the timeless charm of black and white film or the instant gratification of digital snapshots, choosing the right photography class can turn your interest into a passion and perhaps even a skill you'll cherish throughout your retirement years.

When selecting a class, aligning it with your skill level and interests is crucial. Start by exploring local community centers, colleges, or dedicated photography schools that offer classes. Many of these institutions provide beginner courses if you're just starting or more advanced workshops if you're looking to refine your skills. Also consider the type of photography that piques your interest—nature, portrait, street, or even abstract photography. Many specialized classes allow you to dive deep into the style or technique that fascinates you most.

Understanding basic photography skills is an essential part of any class. Key areas typically include mastering camera settings, understanding lighting, and learning about composition. These foundational skills are crucial as they affect the quality and impact of your photographs. For instance, getting to know your camera's settings, such as aperture, shutter speed, and ISO, can dramatically change how your photos look and feel.

Aperture affects the depth of field in your pictures, controlling how much of your shot is in focus. Shutter speed can freeze a fast-moving object or blur a waterfall, conveying motion in your images. ISO impacts the camera's sensitivity to light, which is key for getting good exposure in different lighting conditions.

Composition involves arranging the elements in your shot to create a balanced and engaging photo. Rules like the Rule of Thirds, where you divide your shot into a grid of nine squares and place important elements along these lines or at their intersections, can transform a flat image into a dynamic one.

Engaging in practical exercises is vital to genuinely integrating what you learn in class. Most photography classes will include hands-on projects, which are fun and crucial for cementing your new skills. These could involve assignments like a photo scavenger hunt, where you capture images that meet specific criteria or themes. Another effective practice is participating in photo walks and guided outings that allow you to practice shooting in different environments and lighting conditions under the guidance of your instructor. These walks can be particularly enlightening, providing real-time feedback and tips tailored to your on-the-spot photos, helping you see and capture the world in ways you might not have considered before.

Sharing your work with others and receiving feedback is an invaluable part of learning. Many classes encourage students to participate in photo-sharing sessions, where you can showcase your work and discuss it with classmates. This not only provides you with constructive feedback but also helps you learn from the perspectives and critiques of others, which can be incredibly insightful.

Additionally, many online forums and photography communities offer opportunities to post your images and receive feedback from a broader audience of photography enthusiasts. Engaging with these communities can be especially rewarding, as it connects you with a supportive network of peers who share your passion for photography, offering inspiration, advice, and encouragement as you continue to explore and grow in your photographic journey.

As you delve into the world of photography, you'll find that it's not just about capturing what you see—it's about sharing **how** you see. Each image you take tells a story, your story, through the lens of your unique perspective, creativity, and experiences. Whether it's the delicate veins in a leaf, the joyful chaos of a street festival, or the tranquil solitude of a sunrise, photography allows you to hold onto those moments, celebrate them, and express the inexpressible. So, grab your camera, enroll in a class that excites you, and start capturing the moments that move you. As you do, you'll develop your skills and create a visual diary reflecting the beauty and breadth of your experiences.

4.5 LEARNING A NEW LANGUAGE AT HOME

Isn't it fascinating to think that today, right from your cozy living room or sunny backyard, you can embark on a linguistic adventure that might once have required living abroad? I have learned to speak four languages throughout my life, mainly due to having lived in three countries. It's fascinating to switch to another language without much effort when needed. Thanks to modern technology and resources, learning a new language has never been more accessible or more enjoyable.

Engaging platforms like Duolingo, Rosetta Stone, and even resources available through your local library make it possible to immerse yourself in a new language without stepping outside your door. Duolingo, for instance, offers bite-sized lessons in the form of games, making it fun and engaging. Its system of earning points for correct answers and moving up levels can be pretty addictive in a good way! Rosetta Stone, known for its immersive method, plunges you directly into the language, which can be thrilling as you begin to understand and engage without the crutch of your native tongue.

Incorporating language practice into your daily routine is key to retention and progress. Think about your usual day—perhaps you have a morning routine of reading the news or a bedtime ritual of listening to music. Why not add on to or switch out some of these activities for their language-learning equivalents? Listen to news podcasts in the language you're learning, or end your day with a song from a country where your new language is spoken. Even setting your smartphone or browser to your target language can be an effective, immersive practice. You'll start picking up new vocabulary simply by navigating your day-to-day tasks.

Cultural immersion at home is another way to enhance your language skills. Dive into the films, music, books, and culinary delights of the cultures associated with the language you are learning. Watching foreign films exposes you to the language. It helps you pick up on cultural nuances, gestures, and expressions that are not always taught in traditional language courses. Cooking a traditional dish from a country whose language you are studying can be a fun and delicious way to connect more deeply with the culture. As you chop, stir, and season, you might find yourself learning new words for ingredients and cooking methods.

Connecting with native speakers is perhaps one of the most effective ways to practice and improve your language skills. Language exchange websites like Tandem or ConversationExchange allow you to meet and practice with native speakers who are looking to learn your language as well. It's a win-win situation—you help them with your native language, and they help you with theirs, all while building new friendships.

Many communities also have cultural associations or meet-up groups that organize events and gatherings. Participating in these can provide real-life practice and the opportunity to use your new language skills in various social situations. Engaging regularly with native speakers not only boosts your language proficiency but also deepens your understanding of the cultural context in which the language is used, giving more power to your learning experience far beyond vocabulary and grammar.

Remember that patience and persistence are your best allies as you continue to explore, practice, and immerse yourself in this endeavour. Language learning is a journey of a thousand miles that begins with a single word. So, whether you're deciphering a menu in a new language, exchanging greetings with a friend from another country, or simply enjoying a foreign film without subtitles, celebrate every small victory along the way. Each word you learn is a step toward mastering a language and embracing and experiencing a world different from your own.

4.6 MUSIC AND INSTRUMENT LESSONS FOR BEGINNERS

Imagine filling your retirement days with the soothing sounds of a piano, a guitar's vibrant strums, or even a violin's melodic tunes. Learning to play a musical instrument is not just an enjoyable pastime; it's a journey into a world of rhythm, harmony, and self-expression. I started playing the piano at age forty-five, so you can certainly begin at sixty-five. We're not aiming for a recital in a concert hall but for personal joy.

When choosing an instrument, consider your musical tastes, physical limitations, and practicality. If you have always been moved by classical music, the piano or violin would be fulfilling. For those who enjoy more contemporary music, learning the guitar or ukulele might be more appealing.

It's also important to consider physical comfort; for instance, the harmonica is lightweight and easy to learn, making it ideal for individuals who might find handling larger instruments challenging. Rental options are also available at many music stores, offering a cost-effective way to try different instruments before deciding on the one that best suits your interests and capabilities.

Finding the right music teacher makes a big difference in your learning experience. Look for instructors who have experience teaching adults, as they will understand the learning pace and challenges unique to older beginners. A good teacher should offer personalized learning paths and be patient, encouraging, and skilled at communicating concepts clearly. You can find teachers through local music schools, community centers, or even online platforms that offer virtual lessons. Don't hesitate to ask potential instructors about their teaching approach and experience. See if you can observe a class or have a trial lesson to gauge if their style matches your learning preferences.

The benefits of learning music extend far beyond the joy of playing your favorite tunes. Engaging regularly with music has been shown to improve memory, enhance coordination, and even reduce stress and anxiety. The process of learning and playing music can also boost your cognitive functions, keeping your mind engaged and active. Physically, it helps refine your motor skills and can be a gentle form of exercise, especially for instruments that require breath control, like woodwinds or certain brass instruments. Additionally, the emotional satisfaction of mastering a musical piece is immensely fulfilling, providing a sense of achievement and boosting your self-esteem.

Participating in music groups or recitals can be a fantastic way to add to your musical journey. Many community centers, music schools, and churches host amateur music ensembles or band nights that welcome musicians of all skill levels. Joining these groups can be a great way to meet new people, share your musical progress, and even challenge yourself in a supportive environment. Whether informal gatherings or more structured recitals, performances offer motivational milestones in your music learning process. They encourage you to practice and perfect your skills. They provide a platform to celebrate and share your growth with friends, family, and fellow music enthusiasts.

As you explore the enriching world of music, remember that every note played and every song learned adds a beautiful layer to your life's soundtrack. Whether mastering chords on a guitar or perfecting scales on a piano, music's discipline, joy, and satisfaction can enchant your retirement years.

So, why not pick an instrument that strikes a chord with your heart, find a teacher who can guide you, and start making music that echoes the rhythm of your soul?

As this chapter on Lifelong Learning and Personal Growth comes to a close, we reflect on the incredible opportunities for growth and joy through community classes, online learning, creative writing, photography, language acquisition, and music. Each of these avenues offers unique ways to expand your horizons, connect with others, continue evolving, and enjoy life to its fullest. As we turn the page, we look forward to exploring more dimensions of a fulfilling retirement, ensuring that every day is lived with purpose, passion, and a zest for new experiences.

CHAPTER 5: ARTS AND CREATIVITY

I magine transforming a simple lump of clay into a beautiful, functional piece of art created by your own hands. Pottery making is a form of expression that connects you to the earth and centuries of craft tradition. As you embark on this journey, each touch and mold of the clay can be therapeutic, offering a creative outlet and a profound sense of accomplishment and relaxation. In this chapter, let's explore how you can dive into the world of pottery, from finding the right workshop to mastering the basic techniques and understanding the enriching benefits of this ancient art form.

5.1 POTTERY MAKING IN LOCAL WORKSHOPS

Finding Local Pottery Workshops

Embarking on your pottery journey begins with finding the right workshop where creativity meets guidance. Local community centers, art schools, and even some colleges often offer pottery classes tailored to a range of skills, including beginners. When searching for the perfect class, consider factors like the size of the class, which ideally should be small, allowing for more personalized instruction and hands-on support from the teacher.

A good workshop will provide all the necessary materials and tools, so you won't need to invest in expensive equipment immediately. To find these workshops, a simple internet search such as "pottery classes near me" can yield results, or you might check local community bulletin boards. Visiting local art fairs and speaking to artists can also lead you to recommendations on where to start your pottery journey.

Basic Techniques and Tools

Once you've found your workshop, you'll begin learning the fundamental techniques of pottery making. Key among these is wedging, a method used to prepare the clay by kneading it to remove air bubbles and ensure a uniform consistency. Think of it like preparing dough for bread, a meditative motion that readies the clay for your creative touch. Next, you'll learn centering, which involves placing the lump of clay in the middle of the pottery wheel, followed by the thrilling process of shaping it as the wheel spins. You'll start with simple forms like cylinders and bowls, gradually moving to more complex shapes as your confidence and skills grow.

Glazing and Firing Processes

After you've shaped your pottery, it's time to add color and finish through glazing and firing. Glazing involves applying a coating of liquid glass that forms a glossy and often colorful finish on your piece when fired in a kiln. This stage allows you to experiment with different colors and textures, adding a personal touch to every piece you create. The firing process hardens the clay and sets the glaze when your pottery is heated to high temperatures. It's a transformative moment, turning your soft clay creation into a sturdy, glass-like object. Safety is paramount at this stage, and a good workshop will guide you through the proper techniques and precautions to ensure a successful firing.

Benefits of Pottery

On a physical level, the act of manipulating clay can improve hand-eye coordination and dexterity. Mentally, the required focus can act as a form of meditation, calming and reducing stress. Emotionally, the satisfaction of creating something beautiful and functional from a mere lump of clay significantly boosts self-esteem and personal satisfaction. Moreover, pottery can be a social activity, providing an opportunity to meet new people and share in a creative endeavor, further enhancing your mental and emotional well-being.

As you immerse yourself in the world of pottery, you'll find that each piece you create is not just an object of art; it's a reflection of your journey, a story shaped by your hands, and a testament to the beauty of transformation. So why not let your creative spirits soar as you mold, shape, and color your visions into reality? The world of pottery awaits, ready to be discovered and cherished.

5.2 SCRAPBOOKING MEMORIES: A STEP-BY-STEP GUIDE

Scrapbooking is more than just sticking photos on a page. This art form that allows you to weave your memories into a story told through images, embellishments, and texts. It not only preserves your cherished moments but also turns memory-keeping into a therapeutic hobby. Let's start with the essentials.

You'll need a good quality scrapbook album and various supplies, including different types of paper, such as cardstock and patterned paper, which are the foundation of your layouts. Adhesives are crucial; opt for photo-safe adhesives like double-sided tape or glue dots that won't damage your photos over time. Scissors are a must, and precision craft scissors can make cutting intricate shapes easier. For those who enjoy adding a bit of flair, punches and decorative scissors shape paper edges and cutouts beautifully.

Now, organizing your photos and memorabilia is the next important step. Begin by selecting a theme for your scrapbook—maybe a family vacation, a milestone birthday, or a first year in retirement. Gather photos and items related to your theme, such as tickets, postcards, or dried flowers. Sort these by date or event to give a chronological structure or by theme to highlight different aspects of the story you want to tell. This helps you plan your layout and ensure your scrapbook tells a coherent and captivating story. Use acid-free photo sleeves or envelopes to store items as you organize them, protecting them from dust and damage throughout your project.

Creating your layouts is where your creativity truly shines. Start with a background paper that complements your theme, then layer on photos and memorabilia. Experiment with different placements before gluing anything down. Techniques like layering, where you stack various elements on top of each other, add depth and interest. Journaling is another vital aspect; it's your chance to add personal stories and details about the photos. Use a fade-resistant pen to write directly on your pages, or type your notes and print them on acid-free paper. Embellishments like stickers, stamps, ribbons, and washi tape not only decorate your pages but also help frame and highlight key elements of your layout.

Finally, preserving these memories properly means using archival-quality materials. This ensures that your scrapbook will last generations without the photos fading or the paper deteriorating. Look for products labeled as acid-free and lignin-free to prevent yellowing and degradation. When your scrapbook is complete, store it in a cool, dry place away from direct sunlight to avoid fading and moisture damage. Keep it in an archival-safe box or sleeve for extra protection if possible. This careful preservation means your scrapbook will remain a vibrant treasury of your life's cherished moments, shared with family and friends for many years to come.

5.3 INTRODUCTION TO DIGITAL PAINTING

Imagine transforming a blank canvas into a vibrant landscape or a striking portrait with just a few clicks and swipes. Digital painting opens up a world of artistic possibilities that combines traditional painting techniques with modern technology, offering a cleaner, more versatile approach to creating art. If you're curious about starting this exciting form of expression, your first steps will involve selecting the right software and tools.

Software and Hardware

For beginners, programs like Adobe Photoshop and Corel Painter offer intuitive interfaces and extensive resources to help you get started. These software options come packed with a variety of brushes and tools that mimic the effects of real-life art materials like oils, watercolors, and pastels. Procreate is another excellent choice for those new to digital art, especially if you prefer working on a tablet. It's user-friendly, relatively affordable, and available on iOS platforms.

When it comes to hardware, investing in a good-quality graphic tablet can significantly enhance your digital painting experience. Wacom tablets are widely praised for their sensitivity and responsiveness, but there are also more budget-friendly options like Huion and XP-Pen that offer a good range of features for beginners. These tablets allow you to draw directly onto a digital surface with a stylus, giving you the feel of traditional drawing and painting but with the convenience and versatility of pressing a button to undo strokes. The pressure-sensitive stylus reacts like a real brush or pencil, providing a natural and intuitive way to create varying lines and textures.

Basic Techniques

Once you have your software and tablet set up, it's time to dive into the basic techniques of digital painting. The fundamental skill of layering lets you create depth in your artwork by stacking different elements on separate layers. This way, you can edit each layer independently without affecting the rest of your painting, making adjustments and corrections much easier than in traditional painting.

Blending is another essential technique, which can be mastered by experimenting with different brush settings and opacities. This skill is crucial for creating smooth transitions and realistic textures in your artwork, as is selecting the right brushes. Each software comes with various brushes designed for specific effects, and learning which brush to use for different aspects of your painting can dramatically affect the style and outcome of your work.

To further enhance your skills, there are numerous tutorials and online resources available that can guide you through more advanced digital painting techniques. Websites like Udemy and Skillshare offer comprehensive courses taught by experienced artists, covering everything from beginner skills to advanced techniques for more seasoned artists. YouTube is another invaluable resource where many artists post free tutorials and step-by-step guides to help you tackle specific projects or learn new methods. These resources improve your technical skills, inspire creativity, and help you develop your unique artistic style.

Community

Sharing your digital artwork can be incredibly rewarding, offering both recognition and feedback that can help you grow as an artist. Platforms like DeviantArt, ArtStation, and Instagram are popular among digital artists for showcasing their work. These communities are great for gaining visibility, connecting with other artists, participating in challenges, and engaging in constructive critiques.

When you share your art, remember to engage with your viewers by responding to comments and participating in discussions. This interaction can lead to more exposure and even opportunities for commissions or collaborations. Sharing your journey and progress can also inspire others who are just starting, making the digital art community a vibrant and supportive space for artists of all levels.

As you venture into the colorful world of digital painting, remember that each piece you create is a reflection of your journey in this art form. With each digital stroke, you craft art, hone your skills, express your vision, and connect with a community that shares your passion. So, pick up your stylus, open your chosen app, and start bringing your digital world of art to life.

5.4 KNITTING AND CROCHETING: BEYOND THE BASICS

Imagine sitting comfortably with a set of knitting needles or a crochet hook in hand, yarn spooling out in vibrant colors as you work it into intricate patterns and designs. Knitting and crocheting are not just hobbies—they're crafts that offer deep satisfaction and a sense of achievement as you progress from simple scarves to more complex projects like lace knitting or amigurumi, the Japanese art of knitting or crocheting small, stuffed yarn creatures. These advanced projects challenge your skills and expand your creative horizons, bringing a delightful complexity to your crafting sessions.

As you grow more confident in basic stitches, you might find yourself drawn to these detailed patterns. Lace knitting, for example, involves creating delicate, openwork designs that can be transformed into elegant shawls, doilies, or even tablecloths. The patterns often require careful attention and counting, providing a satisfying challenge with a beautiful result.

On the other hand, amigurumi invites you to the whimsical world of creating adorable stuffed animals, characters, and objects. This type of crochet hooks you into sculpting yarn into three-dimensional shapes, often imbued with character and charm. While these projects seem daunting, they are feasible with patience and practice. Many craft stores and libraries offer pattern books specifically for these types of knitting and crocheting, and countless resources are available online, including step-by-step tutorials and video guides that can help you master these advanced techniques.

Joining a knitting or crocheting group provides a wealth of knowledge and experience, where members share techniques, patterns, and advice. Whether you join a local meet-up or an online community, the support and inspiration you find among fellow crafters can be invaluable. These groups often participate in larger projects, such as making blankets for local shelters or hats for hospital patients, allowing you to work on a bigger project than you might tackle on your own. Additionally, many groups offer workshops or classes focused on specific techniques or projects, providing a structured learning environment along with the camaraderie of like-minded individuals.

The choice of yarn and tools also plays a crucial role as you delve into more advanced knitting and crocheting. The variety of yarns available today is vast, each with different textures and properties. For delicate lace patterns, lightweight, fibrous yarns like mohair or silk blends offer finesse and detail, while sturdy cotton or wool yarns are perfect for amigurumi, providing the necessary structure and durability. Tools such as circular needles or different crochet hook sizes can offer new possibilities for approaching a project. Circular needles, for example, are great for projects with many stitches, like blankets or circular garments, as they hold all your stitches more comfortably and distribute weight more evenly.

Beyond the joy of creating, knitting and crocheting also offer significant therapeutic benefits. The rhythmic nature of knitting and crocheting has been shown to help reduce anxiety and stress, much like meditation. The focus required can also provide a mental break from daily worries, creating a sense of calm and mindfulness. Physically, these activities can help maintain fine motor skills and hand-eye coordination. When completing a complex pattern or learning a new stitch, the sense of accomplishment can boost self-esteem and provide a tangible reward for your effort and patience.

As you continue to explore the vast and varied world of knitting and crocheting, remember that each stitch is a step toward mastering a craft and a form of personal expression and relaxation. The projects you create are not just items but reflections of your creativity and dedication, woven and stitched with care. So, pick up those needles or hooks, choose a challenging pattern, and let your creativity flow into every loop and stitch.

5.5 WRITING POETRY FOR PERSONAL REFLECTION

With its many forms and structures, poetry offers a unique way for you to express your deepest emotions and thoughts, often in ways that prose cannot capture. Whether you're drawn to the structured beauty of a sonnet or the succinct and powerful haiku, each poetic form brings its own rhythm and voice to your experiences.

With their fourteen lines and strict rhyme schemes, traditional sonnets challenge you to express complex feelings within a disciplined framework, often leading to profound revelations and a strong emotional punch. Haiku, rooted in Japanese tradition, requires capturing a moment or emotion in just three lines, focusing on vivid imagery and natural elements to evoke deeper meanings. Free verse, unbound by rhyme or meter, offers the freedom to break traditional boundaries and flow with your thoughts, providing a liberating platform for personal expression.

When you begin writing poetry, try to let your emotions guide your words. Start by jotting down feelings, thoughts, or memories that resonate with you. Don't worry about form or structure initially; let your mind wander and your pen flow. As your ideas take shape, you can mold them into the poetic form that best suits the tone and emotion you wish to convey. For instance, if you're dealing with a particularly intense or precise emotion, a sonnet's structured format might help you distill those feelings into powerful, concentrated expressions. Alternatively, if your thoughts are more expansive or free-flowing, free verse could be the perfect canvas for your reflections.

Local or online poetry workshops serve as invaluable resources as you delve deeper into the world of poetry. These workshops provide a supportive environment where you can share your work and receive feedback from fellow poets and experienced instructors. The collaborative atmosphere encourages learning and growth as you discover new techniques and perspectives to enhance your poetic skills. Many community centers, libraries, and online platforms host regular workshops and poetry slams that welcome poets of all levels. Participating in these events boosts your confidence and helps you refine your craft through constructive critique and encouragement.

Publishing Poetry

Sharing your poetry can be as rewarding as writing it, allowing you to connect with others through your words and experiences. Today, there are numerous avenues available for publishing poetry, each offering different opportunities to reach readers. Community newsletters and local newspapers often welcome contributions from local poets, providing a platform to share your work with a community-connected audience. Online blogging platforms like WordPress and social media sites like Instagram have emerged as popular venues for poets to publish their work.

These platforms offer the advantage of reaching a global audience, allowing you to engage with readers from all over the world. For a more formal approach, self-publishing platforms like Amazon's Kindle Direct Publishing let you publish your poetry collections electronically or as print-on-demand books, giving you complete control over the publishing process and the potential to earn royalties from your work.

Whether you share your poetry with close friends through a personal blog or aspire to reach a wider audience by self-publishing a collection, publishing your work can be deeply fulfilling. It not only validates your experiences and emotions but also invites readers to share in your journey, creating connections that transcend the individual and resonate with the universal human experience. As you explore the various forms and forums for your poetry, remember that each line you write and share reflects your unique perspective, a gift of insight and emotion that enriches the tapestry of human expression.

5.6 DIY HOME DECOR PROJECTS

Transforming your home with your creations personalizes your space and brings an immense sense of achievement and joy. DIY home decor projects are perfect if you love adding a personal touch to your environment without needing extensive tools or materials. Let's start with some simple projects you can dive into immediately.

Painting old furniture can give new life to your favorite but worn pieces. Choose a color that complements your room, or go bold with a vibrant hue. This project requires just a few supplies—sandpaper, a good quality paintbrush, and furniture paint. Creating photo frames from scratch or embellishing existing ones can also be a rewarding project. Use materials like old magazines, fabric scraps, or sea shells to add a unique touch. Another enjoyable project is making decorative pillows. With basic sewing skills, you can create custom pillows that match your decor or serve as statement pieces.

Sustainable crafting is a creative challenge and an environmentally friendly approach to DIY projects. Consider using recycled or upcycled materials to create beautiful home decorations. For instance, you can transform old jars into chic vases or candle holders with just some string and paint. Old clothes can be repurposed into beautiful quilts or curtains, giving them a new life. You can also refurbish furniture destined for the landfill and convert them into stunning, functional pieces. This approach saves money and helps reduce waste, making your crafting hobby a boon for the environment.

Safety and ergonomics are crucial when engaging in any form of DIY project. Always work in a well-ventilated area, especially when painting or using any form of chemicals. Wear protective gear such as gloves or masks when necessary. Ensure your workspace is set up to prevent strain. If you're working on projects that require you to sit or stand for long periods, take regular breaks and stretch. If sewing or knitting, use a chair that supports your back comfortably and a table at the right height to avoid hunching over.

Community projects offer a fantastic opportunity to extend your crafting passion beyond your home. Participating in art installations or community beautification projects can be incredibly fulfilling. These activities allow you to contribute positively to your community and connect with like-minded individuals. Many communities have art councils or local groups that organize events such as mural painting or garden beautification that welcome volunteers. Such involvement beautifies public spaces, strengthens community bonds, and fosters a sense of pride and ownership among its members.

As we wrap up this chapter on Arts and Creativity, reflect on the infinite ways you can express yourself artistically, whether it's through the tactile joy of pottery, the preservation of memories through scrapbooking, the innovative realm of digital painting, the rhythmic pleasure of knitting and crocheting, or the profound expression found in poetry.

Each of these crafts provides unique tools to enhance your personal spaces, growth, and community connections. Next, we will explore the enriching world of social and community activities, where your new skills and crafts can play a significant role in enhancing not only your life but also the lives of those around you.

MAKE A DIFFERENCE

UNLOCK THE POWER OF GENEROSITY

"Sharing your joy doubles it"

People who give without expectation live longer, happier lives. So, if we have a chance to spread some joy during our time together, let's go for it!

<u>To make that happen, I have a question for you...</u>

Would you help someone you've never met, even if you never got credit for it?

Who is this person, you ask? They are like you. Or, at least, like you used to be. Less experienced in their newfound freedom, wanting to explore the possibilities of retirement, and needing guidance but not sure where to start.

My mission is to make *Your Ultimate Retirement Adventure* accessible to everyone.

This is where you come in. Most people do, in fact, judge a book by its cover (and its reviews). So here's my ask on behalf of a curious new retiree you've never met:

Please help that new retiree by leaving this book a review.

Your gift costs no money and takes less than 60 seconds to make real, but it can change a fellow post-work adventurer's life forever. Your review could help…

…one more retiree discover exciting hobbies
…one more person find joy in new activities
…one more individual gain confidence in their post-work life

...one more person make unforgettable memories
...one more dream come true.

To get that 'feel good' feeling and help this person for real, all you have to do is...leave a review.

Simply scan the QR code with your smartphone to leave your review, OR click the following link. Either way you get to the book's review page on Amazon:

https://www.amazon.com/review/review-your-purchases/?asin=B0DFJ3CXD4

If you feel good about helping a faceless, like-minded new retiree, you are my kind of person. Welcome to the club. You're one of us.

I'm that much more excited to help you get the most wonderful post-work life faster and easier than you can possibly imagine. You'll love the ideas and activities I'm about to share in the coming chapters.

Thank you from the bottom of my heart.

Now, back to the new and unexpected adventures you can make part of your new life.

Alan Turner

CHAPTER 6: SOCIAL CONNECTIONS AND COMMUNITY BUILDING

I magine transforming your passion for reading into an engaging social activity that connects you with friends and fellow enthusiasts. Book clubs are vibrant communities that thrive on shared experiences, diverse perspectives, and the love of literature. Whether you're a fan of thrilling mysteries, heartfelt dramas, or insightful non-fiction, starting a book club in retirement can be a wonderful way to meet new people, stimulate your mind, and enjoy meaningful discussions. Let's explore how you can create a successful book club that becomes a highlight of your social calendar.

6.1 STARTING A BOOK CLUB: A GUIDE FOR RETIREES

Choosing the Right Books

Selecting the right books is crucial to the success of your book club. The ideal book selection should cater to diverse tastes and provoke thoughtful discussion. Consider a mix of genres and themes to keep the engagements dynamic and inclusive. For instance, alternating between fiction and non-fiction can serve the varied interests and provide fresh topics for discussion at each meeting. Historical novels can offer a window into different cultures and periods, while contemporary issues in non-fiction can spark conversations about modern-day challenges and perspectives.

When choosing books, it's also worthwhile to consider the length and complexity of the books. Lean toward books that aren't too long, ensuring all members have time to read them between meetings without feeling overwhelmed. Additionally, it can be helpful to choose books that are widely available in libraries, bookstores, or online platforms so all members can access them easily. Occasionally, you might also explore books that have been adapted into movies or TV shows. Watching the adaptation together can be a delightful activity, followed by a discussion of the differences between the book and its screen version, adding an extra layer of interest to your meetings.

Setting Up and Organizing Meetings

The logistics of your book club meetings are important to keep the club running smoothly. Decide early on the frequency of meetings —monthly meetings are common, giving members enough time to read the book without feeling rushed. Choosing a convenient location is also key; rotating between members' homes can add a personal touch and comfort, or you might select a local library, community center, or even a quiet café that supports local book clubs.

Establishing a reliable communication channel is essential for organizing and reminding members about meetings. Tools like email, WhatsApp groups, or social media platforms can effectively send updates, share thoughts, or even discuss logistics. Make sure everyone is comfortable with the chosen method of communication and keep everyone informed about upcoming books and meetings.

Discussion Leading Techniques

Leading a book discussion effectively helps all members feel engaged and valued. Start each meeting with a summary of the book to refresh memories and set the stage for discussion. Prepare a list of open-ended questions encouraging members to express their opinions and interpretations rather than just stating facts. These questions might explore the characters' motivations, the relevance of the book's themes to modern-day issues, or personal connections to the story.

Encourage all members to participate by gently inviting quieter members to share their thoughts and ensuring that more talkative members don't dominate the conversation. It's essential to foster a respectful and open atmosphere where differing opinions are welcomed and discussed thoughtfully. Sometimes, discussions can veer off track, so having a designated moderator for each meeting can help steer the conversation back to the book.

Expanding the Club

As your book club grows, consider ways to keep it vibrant and engaging. Inviting new members can bring fresh perspectives and ideas to discussions. Consider contacting the local community through libraries or community bulletin boards to find potential members who share your passion for reading.

Integrating guest speakers, such as local authors or literary experts, can provide valuable insights and add a unique element to your meetings. If possible, choose speakers who can provide background information on the book's setting, themes, or historical context, or who might offer a professional critique that deepens the discussion.

Starting a book club in retirement can transform your reading habit into a rich social experience that brings laughter, learning, and connection into your life. With the right books, organized meetings, practical discussions, and a touch of creativity in expanding your club, you're set to embark on a literary adventure that enriches your retirement in unimaginable ways. So gather your fellow readers, pick your first book, and let the pages turn and the conversations flow in the very first meeting of a book club that could soon become the heart of your social life.

6.2 HOW TO ORGANIZE COMMUNITY POTLUCKS

Imagine the joy of gathering with friends, neighbors, and new acquaintances over a shared meal where everyone contributes something to the table. Organizing a community potluck can be a delightful way to foster connections and create a sense of belonging within your community.

The first step in bringing this vision to life is selecting a convenient date and location for most people. Consider a local community center, a park with adequate shelter, or even a large backyard. Verify the chosen venue has sufficient seating and amenities like restrooms and possibly a kitchen for last-minute preparations or warming dishes. Once the date and venue are set, the next crucial task is coordinating the dishes. You want a varied and sufficient spread of appetizers, main courses, desserts, and beverages. Utilizing online tools like sign-up sheets where guests can list what they're bringing helps prevent duplication and manage the menu effectively.

Promoting inclusivity at your potluck is vital so everyone enjoys the gathering. This means considering various dietary restrictions and preferences. When setting up the online sign-up sheet, encourage your guests to note if their dish meets specific dietary needs, such as gluten-free, vegan, or nut-free. This thoughtful approach makes everyone feel included and makes it easier for guests to navigate their choices during the potluck. To make everyone feel even more welcome, consider labeling the dishes with ingredients at the potluck, which is especially helpful for those with allergies or dietary restrictions.

Incorporating activities and entertainment brings addition fun and togetherness to your potluck. Simple games like charades or trivia can break the ice and get everyone mingling. If space and resources allow, setting up a small stage for local musicians or speakers can add a delightful ambiance to the gathering. Storytelling is another beautiful activity where guests can share funny or heartwarming stories related to food and community. These activities provide entertainment and help forge stronger connections among attendees, making the potluck an event to remember.

Safety is paramount in activities, especially when it involves food. Brief all participants on safe food handling and encourage them to prepare dishes under hygienic conditions. On the day of the potluck, arrange to have facilities available for keeping hot foods hot and cold foods cold, which is crucial to avoid foodborne illnesses. If your potluck is outdoors, plan for inclement weather and ensure the location is safe and accessible for everyone, including those with mobility issues. By meticulously planning and considering these details, you ensure that the potluck is not only enjoyable but also a safe gathering for all participants.

6.3 VOLUNTEERING: GIVING BACK TO THE COMMUNITY

Volunteering is a wonderful way to add purpose and joy to your life after retirement. With a wealth of life experience and more free time, you're uniquely equipped to offer valuable contributions to various causes and organizations. The key is finding volunteering opportunities that align with your interests and abilities, so your efforts feel rewarding and impactful.

Start by exploring local nonprofits, schools, and community centers, as they often seek volunteers for different programs and events. Many cities have volunteer centers or websites dedicated to connecting volunteers with opportunities. Consider what you enjoy doing and how you want to make a difference. Whether it's helping children learn to read, participating in environmental clean-ups, or assisting at a local food bank, there's likely an opportunity that matches your passion.

Volunteering offers numerous benefits that go beyond the simple satisfaction of helping others. Engaging in volunteer work can lead to significant skill development. For instance, if you volunteer to help organize a public event, you might hone project management and public speaking skills. Likewise, volunteering at a museum can enhance your knowledge of art and history while enriching visitors' experience. The social connections made through volunteering are also invaluable. Regular interaction with fellow volunteers and community members can lead to lasting friendships and a deeper connection to your community. Moreover, the psychological boost from making a meaningful impact cannot be underestimated. Studies have shown that volunteering can lead to lower levels of stress, increased mental stimulation, and a greater sense of life satisfaction.

When choosing how to engage with volunteer work, consider the commitment level that best suits your lifestyle. Some prefer long-term commitments, which might involve a consistent weekly schedule, offering a steady and reliable way to build relationships and impact. These roles often come with increased responsibility, such as managing a program or leading a team, which can be incredibly fulfilling if you're looking for a deep dive into a cause you're passionate about.

On the other hand, one-time events or short-term projects are ideal if you prefer flexibility or wish to explore various volunteering opportunities before making a longer commitment. These can range from a day of helping at a community fair to a few weeks of working on a specific project. Both types of engagements have their merits, and many volunteers find a combination of the two suits them best, allowing for both regular involvement and the flexibility to explore new opportunities.

Sharing your volunteering experiences with others can amplify the benefits of your work by spreading awareness and inspiring more people to get involved. Consider sharing stories and photos from your volunteering activities with friends and family through social media, email, or even casual conversations. You might also write about your experiences in community newsletters or blogs. Sharing highlights the valuable work being done, encourages a culture of giving, and might inspire others to volunteer. Additionally, discussing your experiences can provide more profound reflections on the impact you're making on others and yourself, reinforcing the value of your contributions and the joy they bring.

6.4 MENTORSHIP OPPORTUNITIES: SHARING YOUR SKILLS

Retirement opens up an excellent opportunity to pass on your wealth of knowledge and experience to others in a meaningful way. Whether you've spent your career in education, engineering, healthcare, or any other field, your skills and insights are invaluable resources that can benefit others. Becoming a mentor allows you to engage deeply in your field or share your life skills, continuing to grow while helping others achieve their potential. Let's explore how you can step into this rewarding role and make a significant impact.

Identifying the right mentoring opportunities often starts with reflecting on what you're passionate about and where you feel you can make the most difference. Many organizations—from startups to nonprofits and educational institutions—look for experienced individuals willing to provide guidance and insight. You can find formal mentoring programs through professional associations related to your career field. These programs often have structures in place that help match mentors with mentees who can benefit the most from your expertise.

Alternatively, informal mentoring can happen naturally, with a younger family member, a neighbor, or a former colleague who is navigating career transitions or major life decisions. The key is to remain open to opportunities where your knowledge and life experiences can serve others, helping them navigate paths you've once walked.

Setting up a successful mentor-mentee relationship involves clear communication from the start. Once you've connected with a mentee, it's vital to establish mutual goals and expectations. Discuss what your mentee hopes to gain from the relationship, and consider what you're willing and able to contribute. Setting these expectations early helps prevent misunderstandings and ensures the relationship is mutually beneficial. It's also important to set boundaries regarding time commitments and meeting formats. Decide how often you will meet and what methods of communication work best for both of you, whether that's face-to-face, over the phone, or through digital platforms. Regular, scheduled interactions help maintain momentum, but flexibility is essential to accommodate the unexpected.

Mentorship is profoundly rewarding for both the mentor and the mentee. For the mentor, the act of guiding someone else is an intellectually stimulating experience that can challenge you to stay current in your field and think critically about why you've made certain decisions in your career or life. It's also deeply fulfilling to see your mentee succeed, knowing you've played a part in their growth and development. For the mentee, having access to a mentor can be transformative. The guidance, encouragement, and advice from someone who has navigated similar challenges can boost their confidence and give them a clearer path to achieving their goals. The relationship often evolves into a lasting connection that enriches both parties' lives beyond the original context of the mentoring.

Expanding your professional and personal networks through mentorship can open up new opportunities and perspectives for both mentor and mentee. As a mentor, you gain insights into the latest industry trends, technologies, and generational perspectives that can invigorate your own thinking and approaches. The mentee gains access to your network of contacts, which can be invaluable for career development and opportunities. This networking aspect can lead to new collaborations, job opportunities, and deeper engagement within your industry or community. Engaging in mentorship also strengthens community ties, creating a culture of support and continuous learning that can have far-reaching benefits.

As you consider stepping into a mentorship role, think of it as a continuation of your professional journey—an opportunity to give back while still growing and learning. It's a chance to leave a legacy of knowledge and wisdom that can shape the careers and lives of others, making a lasting impact that extends well beyond your retirement years. Whether you engage in a formal program or simply share advice informally, the experience of mentoring can be one of the most satisfying and impactful aspects of your life in retirement.

6.5 JOINING LOCAL THEATER GROUPS

Imagine stepping into a world where every scene is a doorway to a new adventure, and every character has a chance to explore a different facet of life. Such is the magic of theater, and it's not just for the young or the professional actors; it's a vibrant community that thrives on diversity and creativity, welcoming individuals from all walks of life, including retirees like you who are eager to try something new or reignite a passion for the dramatic arts. Exploring local theater options can be one of the most exhilarating parts of your post-retirement activities, offering entertainment and a platform for personal expression and community involvement.

To begin, start by researching community theaters in your area and acting troupes that focus on or welcome senior members. Many communities boast groups that encourage participation from retirees, recognizing the depth of experience and the wealth of time that you bring. These groups often advertise in local newspapers, community bulletin boards, or online community forums. Feel free to reach out to them directly or attend performances to get a feel for the troupe's style and camaraderie. Additionally, some groups are dedicated explicitly to senior theater, focusing on plays and productions that are particularly relevant or accommodating to older actors and audiences. These can be fantastic opportunities to engage with peers who share a similar zest for life and a passion for performance.

Theater isn't just about acting. There are numerous roles beyond the spotlight that might pique your interest and utilize your skills. For those who prefer not to perform or want to start gently, roles in costume design offer a creative outlet that contributes significantly to the magic of theater. Costume designers work closely with directors and actors to create outfits that bring characters to life, and this can be a wonderfully fulfilling role for those with a flair for fashion or sewing. Set construction is another critical area where your practical skills can make a tangible impact. Building and painting sets can be pretty rewarding and offers a more behind-the-scenes approach. Additionally, many community theaters need help with administration, from managing ticket sales to promoting performances. These tasks are crucial for the success of any production and can be a great fit if you have organizational skills or a background in business.

Participating in theater can have profound social and cognitive benefits. Engaging in rehearsals and performances is a fantastic way to meet new people and strengthen social ties, which is an essential aspect of maintaining your social health in retirement.

The collaborative nature of theater fosters a strong sense of community and belonging as you work closely with a diverse group of individuals toward the common goal of putting on a great performance. Moreover, it can significantly boost your self-confidence and public speaking skills. Memorizing lines, understanding characters, and performing in front of an audience can enhance your memory and concentration skills, keeping your mind sharp. The cognitive challenge of learning new roles and the physical activity often involved in productions can contribute to your overall mental and physical health.

The idea of participating in public performances may seem daunting, but it is undoubtedly rewarding. Showcases and plays are not only about displaying your new skills; they're celebrations of hard work and community spirit. Whether a small role or a lead, each performance lets you step outside your comfort zone and experience the thrill of live theater. Public performances also contribute significantly to the local cultural scene, adding vibrancy and diversity to community events. By taking part, you enrich your life and bring joy and culture to those around you, enhancing the community's appreciation for the arts and its senior members' contributions.

As you explore the exciting world of local theater, remember that every role, whether on stage or behind the curtains, is a pathway to new friendships, new challenges, and immense personal growth. So why not take a step into the spotlight or lend your skills backstage? The local theater community awaits with open arms, ready to welcome you to an exciting world of drama and camaraderie.

6.6 DANCE CLASSES FOR FUN AND FRIENDSHIP

Picture yourself gliding across the dance floor, laughter mingling with music, surrounded by old and new friends. Dance classes offer a delightful blend of physical activity and social interaction, making them perfect for enriching your retirement years. With a variety of dance styles available, each offering its unique rhythm and flair, you can find the perfect match for your interests and physical capabilities.

For instance, ballroom dancing pairs classic elegance with a structured approach that can be both challenging and deeply rewarding. Salsa, with its lively beats and vibrant movements, is perfect if you're looking for something more upbeat. Meanwhile, line dancing provides a fun, communal experience that doesn't require a partner, making it easy to join in no matter your circumstances.

Finding the right dance class involves considering several factors to get the most out of it. Start by assessing necessary physical fitness—some dance styles might be more demanding than others. It's important to choose a class that matches your current fitness level and mobility. Please don't shy away from discussing with instructors their experience with teaching students of your age group. They can provide valuable insights into what the class involves and how they can modify movements to suit your needs. The class size also matters; smaller groups often allow for more personalized instruction and can make stepping into a new environment less daunting.

The health benefits of dancing are as extensive as they are exciting. Physically, regular participation in dance can improve balance and coordination, which are crucial for maintaining mobility and preventing falls. The varied movements in dancing strengthen your cardiovascular health, boosting heart function and circulation. Additionally, the mental focus required to learn and remember dance steps can act as a cognitive workout, aiding in keeping your mind sharp. Dancing also serves as an effective stress reliever. The combination of physical activity, music, and social interaction can significantly lift your spirits and reduce feelings of depression or anxiety.

Social dance events and themed dance nights create perfect opportunities to practice new skills in a joyful, relaxed environment. These events often feature a variety of music and dance styles, offering a taste of different cultures and communities. They also provide a social platform that extends beyond the classes, helping you build and maintain new friendships. Participation in these events encourages a sense of community and belonging, as you regularly meet up with fellow enthusiasts to enjoy an evening filled with fun and dance. Whether it's a salsa night by the beach or a glamorous ballroom evening, each event offers a new experience to look forward to.

As you step into the world of dance, you join a community that celebrates life through movement and music. Dance classes offer a unique combination of health benefits, lifelong learning, and social interaction, making them a fantastic addition to a fulfilling retirement. So why not put on your dancing shoes and step into a class? Whether it's the elegance of ballroom, the energy of salsa, or the community feel of line dancing, there's a style waiting to sweep you off your feet.

In wrapping up this chapter on Social Connections and Community Building, we've explored a variety of activities that foster connections, enhance well-being, and bring joy into your retirement years. From starting a book club that celebrates the love of reading to dancing the night away with friends, each activity offers unique opportunities to enrich your life and strengthen your community ties.

As we close this chapter, remember that each step you take—whether it's through the pages of a book, across the dance floor, or within your community—builds a richer, more connected retirement. Let these experiences inspire you to continue exploring, learning, and growing in the chapters to come.

CHAPTER 7: HEALTH AND WELL-BEING

I magine your body as a well-tuned orchestra, each part playing in perfect harmony. But as time passes, the instruments might need a little tuning. The same is true with our nutritional needs as we age; what worked for us in our forties or fifties might need adjustments as we mature. Embracing this new phase of life with a tailored approach to eating can significantly improve your overall health, vitality, and joy in daily activities. Let's delve into how you can nourish your body with the right nutrients, plan wholesome meals that tickle your taste buds, understand the language of food labels, and keep hydration in check to remain well-fed and well-fueled for the adventures ahead.

7.1 NUTRITIONAL EATING FOR AGING BODIES

Understanding Nutritional Needs

As we age, our bodies undergo various changes that can affect how we process nutrients, leading to altered dietary requirements. For instance, your metabolism may slow down, decreasing the body's energy needs but not necessarily diminishing its nutrient requirements. Calcium and Vitamin D become crucial for maintaining bone health and reducing the risk of fractures, a common concern as bones weaken with age. Similarly, dietary fiber becomes a star player in maintaining digestive health, which can often become sluggish. Adequate protein intake is essential for preserving muscle mass, which tends to decrease with age, affecting balance and overall activity levels.

Focusing on these nutrients helps in managing the physical aspects of aging and supports cognitive health. For example, omega-3 fatty acids found abundantly in fish like salmon and in flaxseeds are vital for brain health and enhance memory and mental functions. Antioxidant-rich foods like berries, dark chocolate, and leafy greens combat oxidative stress and inflammation, potentially lowering the risk of chronic diseases such as Alzheimer's and heart disease. Emphasizing a diet rich in these nutrients—coupled with reduced sodium and unhealthy fats—can significantly boost your health and allow you to enjoy your retirement years with vitality.

Planning Healthy Meals

Crafting nutritious, easy-to-prepare, and appealing meals might seem like a balancing act, but it can be simplified with some planning. Start by creating a weekly meal plan that incorporates a variety of food groups so you get a balanced mix of the necessary nutrients. For breakfast, think about oatmeal topped with a sprinkle of flaxseeds and fresh berries, offering a hearty dose of fiber and antioxidants. Lunch could be a vibrant salad with leafy greens, nuts, and grilled chicken, dressed lightly with olive oil and lemon, providing a good mix of protein, healthy fats, and vitamins.

For dinners, focus on incorporating lean protein sources like fish or tofu, as well as whole grains, such as quinoa and brown rice, along with steamed vegetables. These meals cater to your nutritional needs and adapt easily to common dietary restrictions among older adults, such as low-sodium or diabetic-friendly diets. If you're managing specific health conditions, consider consulting with a dietitian who can help tailor your meal plans further to get the most out of your diet.

Reading Food Labels

Navigating the world of food labels can be like deciphering a new language. However, understanding these can empower you to make healthier choices. Start by looking at the serving size, which can often be misleading; ensure that your portion corresponds to the serving size listed. Next, check the calories and nutrients. Focus on the amounts of dietary fiber, protein, vitamins, and minerals, aiming for higher values of these. Be wary of sodium, sugars, and saturated fats, which should ideally be low. Also, pay attention to the ingredient list—fewer ingredients usually indicate a less processed food. Look for whole foods that are closer to their natural state.

Staying Hydrated

Hydration is crucial, yet it's often overlooked. As we age, our sense of thirst may diminish, increasing the risk of dehydration. This can lead to various health issues, including urinary tract infections, constipation, and even confusion. To ensure adequate fluid intake, drink at least eight glasses of water daily, more if you're active or it's a hot day. Keep a water bottle handy throughout the day as a reminder to drink regularly. Remember, fluids come not only from water but also from other beverages and high-water-content foods like cucumbers, tomatoes, and watermelons. Herbal teas are also a great option, providing hydration without caffeine.

By embracing these nutritional strategies, you can significantly enhance your well-being and feed your body the right fuel to thrive during your retirement years. Enjoy the process of exploring new foods and recipes that align with your health goals, making each meal a step toward sustained health and vitality.

7.2 MEDITATION AND MINDFULNESS PRACTICES

Imagine starting your day with a calm mind and a serene heart, carrying that tranquility through every task and interaction. Meditation and mindfulness can be your gateway to this peaceful existence, helping you cultivate mental clarity and reduce stress. If you're new to these practices, don't worry; the beauty of meditation lies in its simplicity and adaptability to individual needs and lifestyles. Let's explore some basic techniques that you can start practicing right from the comfort of your home.

Focused breathing is one of the simplest yet most powerful forms of meditation. It involves concentrating on your breath, observing each inhale and exhale without trying to change the rhythm. Initially counting your breaths can prevent your mind from wandering. Guided imagery, another beginner-friendly technique, involves visualizing a peaceful scene—perhaps a quiet beach at sunset or a serene path through a forest. These mental images can promote a sense of calm and relaxation. The benefits of these practices are profound, ranging from enhanced mental clarity to significant stress reduction and even improvements in physical health, such as lowered blood pressure and improved sleep patterns.

Incorporating mindfulness into your daily activities can transform mundane tasks into moments of calm reflection and joy. Mindful walking is a beautiful way to start; it involves paying close attention to the experience of walking, noticing the sensation of your feet touching the ground, the rhythm of your breath, and the sounds around you. Try this during your morning walk and observe how it turns a routine exercise into a refreshing mindfulness practice. Similarly, mindful eating involves:

- Savoring each bite
- Being fully present as you eat
- Appreciating the flavors and textures of your food

This practice enhances your culinary experience, aids digestion, and promotes satisfaction with smaller portions.

Tools and Apps to Assist Practice

Many tools and apps are available to help you maintain consistency in your meditation and mindfulness practices. Apps like Headspace and Calm offer guided meditation sessions that can be tailored to your schedule and preferences while featuring a variety of meditation types that cater to different goals like reducing anxiety or enhancing focus.

These apps often include progress trackers and personalized tips, making it easier for beginners to start and sustain their practice. Additionally, consider using a journal to record your experiences and reflections. It can help you understand your progress, notice patterns in your thoughts or feelings, and adjust your practice to better suit your needs.

<u>Overcoming Common Challenges</u>

It's normal to encounter some hurdles when you begin meditating. Distraction is one of the most common challenges; you might find your mind wandering to chores, work, or other concerns. When this happens, gently acknowledge the distraction and guide your focus to your breath or the guided imagery. This redirection of attention is itself a practice of mindfulness. Impatience can also arise, especially if you're eager to experience benefits quickly. Remember, meditation is a skill that develops over time, and its benefits are cumulative. Be kind to yourself and recognize that each session is a step toward greater mindfulness and health.

It's also important to realize that whatever comes up during meditation is okay. The point is not to judge anything or let yourself get annoyed. Your awareness should be in the 'now', and whatever is there is there. Once you stop fighting what comes up - like your mind wandering off - it tends to happen less frequently. Allowing everything is key.

As you integrate these practices into your life, you'll find that meditation and mindfulness are not just tasks to be completed but enjoyable experiences that enrich your daily living. They offer a sanctuary of peace that you can carry within you, transforming how you interact with the world around you.

7.3 MANAGING CHRONIC CONDITIONS WITH SMART HABITS

Living with a chronic condition doesn't have to define your retirement years. Instead, it can be an opportunity to fine-tune your lifestyle, embrace habits that manage your condition, and enhance your overall quality of life. From keeping a close watch on your symptoms and medications to making small yet impactful lifestyle changes, the strategies you adopt can make a significant difference. Let's explore how you can proactively manage common chronic conditions like diabetes, heart disease, and arthritis so they don't keep you from enjoying your golden years.

Daily management of chronic conditions involves meticulously monitoring your health and adhering to treatments. For instance, if you're managing diabetes, regularly monitoring your blood glucose levels is critical. A home glucose monitor can help you keep track of your sugar levels and understand how different foods, activities, and medications affect your condition. Similarly, keeping tabs on your blood pressure and cholesterol levels can help prevent complications when dealing with heart disease.

People with arthritis might benefit from daily journals that track pain levels, weather changes, and physical activity, helping identify triggers or effective relief methods. Medication management is another crucial aspect. Organizing your medications using a pill organizer makes taking the proper doses at the correct times easier, and setting reminders on your phone or clock can help you maintain this routine without fail.

Lifestyle adjustments are often necessary when you're living with chronic conditions. Still, they can also be opportunities to rediscover your health. Quitting smoking, for example, is a powerful way to improve your heart and lung health, reducing symptoms and complications associated with chronic respiratory or cardio-vascular diseases. Moderating alcohol consumption can also have a beneficial effect on your overall health, particularly for those managing diabetes or hypertension, as excessive drinking can exacerbate these conditions.

Increasing your physical activity level is another beneficial change. Even gentle exercises like walking or swimming can improve cardiovascular health, increase joint flexibility, and boost mood. Always consult your healthcare provider before starting any new exercise regimen to ensure it's safe and appropriate for your health needs.

Regular monitoring using self-assessment tools plays a pivotal role in managing chronic conditions effectively. Many health devices and apps can help you track vital health metrics at home. Blood pressure monitors, wearable fitness trackers, and mobile health apps provide valuable data that can help you and your healthcare provider make informed decisions about your healthcare. These tools can also help you recognize early signs of potential health issues, enabling timely medical intervention that can prevent complications.

Always prepare for doctor's appointments with a list of questions or concerns about your condition. This preparation ensures you make the most of your time with your healthcare provider and receive the guidance you need. Don't hesitate to ask for clarification if you're unsure about any advice or instructions your doctor provides, including about medications or treatments.

Telemedicine has become a valuable resource for many seniors, offering a convenient way to consult with your doctor without the need to travel. Familiarize yourself with telemedicine and consider it a viable option for routine check-ups or consultations, especially if mobility or transportation is challenging.

By embracing these strategies, you can take control of your health and continue to lead a fulfilling and active life, even with chronic conditions. Remember, small daily actions can lead to substantial health benefits, and every positive change you make contributes to a healthier, happier you.

7.4 THE IMPORTANCE OF REGULAR CHECK-UPS

Keeping up with regular check-ups is like giving your car a routine service; it might run fine without it, but tuning it regularly can prevent future problems and keep it running smoothly. Regular visits with your healthcare provider are imperative to managing existing conditions and catching potential health issues early. To make the most out of these visits, it's essential to schedule them at intervals recommended by your doctor, which for many might be once or twice a year unless you have conditions that require more frequent monitoring.

When scheduling your appointments, consider times of the year when you're less likely to have other commitments. Setting appointments around the same time each year, such as around a birthday, can help you remember them. Most medical offices now offer various scheduling methods, including online platforms, which can be particularly convenient. You can see available slots in real time and choose one without having to call the office. Before your appointment, prepare a list of topics you want to discuss. This could include symptoms you've noticed, effects of new medications, or questions about diet or exercise. Bringing a list helps you remember all important points during the conversation with your healthcare provider.

You can expect to undergo basic screenings crucial for senior health during your check-up. Blood pressure checks are standard, as hypertension is prevalent among older adults and can occur without any noticeable symptoms. Managing your blood pressure can prevent various complications, from heart disease to kidney problems. Cholesterol levels are another key focus, as high cholesterol can go unnoticed until it leads to more serious heart conditions.

These screenings typically involve a quick and painless blood test. Depending on your age, health history, and family history, your doctor might also recommend cancer screenings such as mammograms, colonoscopies, or skin checks. Understanding what each test or screening entails and what the results mean can help you feel more prepared and less anxious about the process.

Vaccinations are another pivotal aspect of your health care, especially because the immune system naturally weakens with age. Staying updated with vaccinations can protect you from severe illnesses. The flu vaccine is recommended annually for older adults, since influenza can be particularly severe in this age group. Pneumonia vaccines are also important, as pneumonia remains a leading cause of death among seniors. Other vaccinations, like shingles or tetanus, might be advised depending on your medical history. Discuss with your doctor which vaccinations are appropriate for you, and keep an immunization schedule to track when you receive each vaccine and when you're due for a booster.

Keeping an organized record of your medical history, test results, medications, and vaccinations can greatly assist in the quality of care you receive, especially if you see multiple specialists or need to visit a new doctor. Consider maintaining a health journal or folder where you keep all your health-related documents. Many also find digital apps helpful for storing this information, often allowing you to share information directly with your healthcare provider. This readily available information can be invaluable in emergencies when quick access to your medical history may be critical.

Regular medical check-ups are a cornerstone of healthy aging, providing a framework for monitoring your health and catching potential problems early. They also offer an excellent opportunity to discuss preventive health measures with your doctor, ensuring you remain active and enjoy a high quality of life as you age. So, take charge of your health by scheduling your next appointment today. Go into each check-up prepared and informed, ready to discuss anything that might help you maintain your best health.

7.5 SLEEP HYGIENE FOR BETTER REST

A good night's sleep is like a reset button for your body and mind, integral for rejuvenating you so you can face each new day with energy and positivity. As we age, achieving restful sleep can become challenging, yet with the right environment and habits, you can significantly enhance your sleep quality. Let's explore how to create a sleep-conducive environment and establish routines that promote sound, restorative sleep.

Creating a space that invites relaxation and sleep involves several key elements, starting with the temperature of your bedroom. The ideal temperature for sleep is around 65 degrees Fahrenheit (18 degrees Celsius). This cooler temperature helps to lower your body's core temperature, signaling that it's time to wind down and drift off. If you find this too cool, adjust it slightly, but remember, overly warm rooms can disrupt sleep.

Lighting also plays a critical role in your sleep environment. Exposure to natural light during the day helps maintain a healthy sleep-wake cycle, but as bedtime approaches, it's beneficial to dim the lights and close the curtains to boost the production of melatonin, the hormone responsible for sleep. To further optimize your bedroom, consider the noise level. If external sounds are a nuisance, a white noise machine can mask disruptive noises with soothing sounds like falling rain or ocean waves, increasing your ability to sleep undisturbed.

In addition to optimizing your environment, establishing a consistent bedtime routine can signal your body that it's time to wind down. This routine might include reading a book, taking a warm bath, or practicing relaxation exercises such as gentle yoga or deep breathing. These activities can help ease the transition from wakefulness to sleep, making falling and staying asleep easier. It's also wise to limit caffeine intake late in the day. Caffeine is a stimulant, and consuming it in the afternoon or evening can keep you alert and delay sleep. Similarly, while alcohol makes you drowsy, it disrupts sleep later in the night, so it's best to avoid it close to bedtime.

Dealing with sleep issues, such as insomnia or frequent waking, can be particularly frustrating. These problems are not uncommon in older adults, often stemming from changes in sleep architecture, health conditions, or medications. If you struggle with sleep, maintaining a sleep diary can be helpful. Record when you go to bed, wake up, and any nighttime awakenings. This record can provide insights into patterns or behaviors affecting your sleep. For instance, late-night snacks or TV time could be interfering with your sleep. If basic adjustments to your sleep habits and environment don't help, it may be time to seek professional advice. Sleep specialists can offer guidance based on your specific circumstances; sometimes, simple treatments or changes to your medication can make a significant difference.

The connection between good sleep and your overall health is profound. Adequate sleep supports various functions, such as memory, mood regulation, and physical health. It plays a critical role in cognitive function, with poor sleep linked to reduced concentration and higher risks of cognitive decline. Physically, sleep is essential for repairing and rejuvenating your heart and blood vessels. Consistent lack of sleep has been associated with a higher risk of heart disease, kidney disease, high blood pressure, and diabetes. Moreover, the impact of good sleep extends to emotional and mental health, helping to combat stress and depression and improve overall life satisfaction.

Addressing these aspects of sleep hygiene creates a foundation for improved sleep, which strengthens physical and mental well-being and boosts the quality of everyday life. Embrace these changes gradually, and you might find yourself sleeping better and enjoying a more vibrant, active life during your waking hours.

7.6 COPING WITH LOSS AND CHANGE

Loss and change are inevitable parts of life, especially as we step into the later chapters, where the pace slows and the landscape shifts. Whether it's the profound grief from the passing of a loved one, the subtle mourning for the loss of independence, or the adjustment to other significant life changes, these experiences shape us profoundly. Recognizing and acknowledging these feelings of loss is the first step toward healing. It's important to understand that grief is not a linear process and can sometimes manifest in various forms—sadness, anger, confusion, or even relief. Allowing yourself to feel these emotions without judgment can be the key to moving through them.

Emotional resilience, the ability to bounce back from such distressing experiences, is key and can be developed through proactive strategies. Staying connected with your community plays an integral role here. Engaging with friends, family, and community groups can provide the support and distraction needed to ease the pain of grief. Additionally, involving yourself in meaningful activities that give you a sense of purpose can be incredibly therapeutic. This might include volunteering, taking up a new hobby, or dedicating time to a long-standing passion. These activities occupy your mind and time and provide moments of joyful satisfaction that can gradually ease the weight of grief.

Support resources play a critical role in navigating the complexities of loss and change. Support groups, whether in person or online, can offer a space to share your experiences and feelings with others who understand what you're going through. This can be immensely comforting and often provides new insights or coping strategies. Counseling services offer professional guidance to help you deal with grief, providing tools to manage emotions and overcome obstacles. Books on coping with loss can also offer comfort and advice. Titles like *On Grief and Grieving* by Elisabeth Kübler-Ross and David Kessler provide profound insights into the nature of grief and healing, helping you understand and process your emotions.

Maintaining a sense of purpose is essential during times of change. It can be easy to feel adrift when life suddenly changes course. By setting goals, however small, and making plans for the future, you can give yourself a sense of direction that helps mitigate feelings of loss. The key is to find enjoyable activities that give you a feeling of accomplishment and contribution. Whether through creative arts, teaching others, or engaging in community service, these activities can help reaffirm your sense of self and purpose, fostering a feeling of belonging and usefulness.

Navigating through loss and change requires patience, support, and proactive engagement in life's activities. By embracing these strategies, you can cultivate resilience and find a renewed sense of joy and purpose in your life, proving that growth and happiness are still achievable even during grief. As this chapter closes, remember that each step you take toward healing and embracing change is a step toward rediscovering your strength and capacity for joy. This journey of renewal is not just about coping with loss but about learning to live with a renewed sense of purpose and fulfillment, paving the way for new experiences and chapters in your life.

CHAPTER 8: FINDING JOY IN EVERYDAY ACTIVITIES

I magine stepping outside into your own little sanctuary, where the air is fresh, the colors vibrant, and the simple act of nurturing life brings an incredible sense of tranquility and accomplishment. Gardening, whether in a sprawling backyard or a modest collection of containers on a balcony, offers a delightful blend of physical activity, mental relaxation, and nutritional benefits. It's a pastime that beautifies your surroundings and nourishes your body and soul.

In this chapter, we explore how you can cultivate a garden of your own, revel in its therapeutic benefits, and enjoy the fruits (and vegetables!) of your labor, all while connecting with nature and others in your community.

8.1 GARDENING FOR RELAXATION AND NUTRITION

Starting a Small Garden

Embarking on your gardening adventure doesn't require vast amounts of space or even previous experience. You can start small; even a few pots or a small patch of land can transform into a flourishing garden. Begin by choosing a location that receives adequate sunlight—a necessary ingredient for plant growth. Most herbs and vegetables need about six to eight hours of direct sunlight daily. If you're working with limited space, consider vertical gardening, utilizing trellises or hanging planters to maximize upward space.

Look for easy-to-grow species that are known for their resilience and low maintenance. Herbs like basil, cilantro, and mint are wonderful starters—they grow relatively quickly and don't require much space. For vegetable gardens, tomatoes, peppers, and lettuce are excellent choices for beginners. They grow well in most climates and provide the rewarding experience of cooking with ingredients you've grown yourself.

Invest in good quality soil when setting up your garden—it's the foundation of healthy plant growth. Look for organic potting mixes at your local garden store, which are often enriched with compost that provides essential nutrients for your plants. As you plant, give each seed or seedling enough room to expand. This prevents overcrowding and promotes better air circulation, reducing the risk of disease. Watering your plants is another crucial aspect, but overwatering can be just as harmful as neglect. Feel the soil about an inch below the surface; it's time to water if it feels dry.

Therapeutic Benefits of Gardening

Gardening is more than just a hobby—it's a form of therapy. Engaging with the earth has been shown to reduce stress, improve mood, and even decrease symptoms of depression and anxiety. Planting, weeding, and harvesting can serve as a mindful practice, keeping you present in the moment and focused on the task at hand. This connection to the present moment helps push aside the worries of tomorrow or the regrets of yesterday.

There's also a physical aspect to gardening that contributes to its therapeutic benefits. Activities like digging, planting, and weeding are gentle forms of exercise that can improve endurance, flexibility, and strength. The sunlight exposure you get while gardening increases your vitamin D levels, which is important for bone health and immune function. Moreover, spending time outdoors is linked to better sleep patterns, likely due to its effects on your body's natural circadian rhythms.

Growing Your Own Food

One of the most rewarding aspects of gardening is the ability to grow your own food. There's a particular pride that comes with eating a meal that includes ingredients you've cultivated with your own hands; it's a direct connection to the earth that's lost in modern food distribution processes. Growing your food isn't just rewarding—it's also healthier. The fruits, vegetables, and herbs you grow yourself are fresher and higher in nutrients than those that have traveled thousands of miles to reach your supermarket shelf.

When planning your garden, consider incorporating a variety of plants that contribute to a balanced diet. Leafy greens such as spinach and kale are rich in vitamins and minerals, particularly iron and calcium. Root vegetables like carrots and beets are high in dietary fiber and vitamin C, essential for digestive health and immunity. Don't forget about herbs—they add flavor to your dishes and have impressive health benefits. For example, rosemary is known for its anti-inflammatory properties, while mint can aid digestion.

If you're interested in organic gardening, start using organic seeds and avoiding synthetic pesticides and fertilizers. Instead, explore natural alternatives like composting, which enriches the soil and reduces waste, and companion planting, which can naturally repel pests. Organic gardening benefits your health and has a lesser impact on the environment.

Gardening Clubs and Community Gardens

Gardening can be a solitary activity, but it also offers terrific opportunities for social interaction. Joining a gardening club or participating in a community garden can expand your social network, provide valuable gardening knowledge, and improve your sense of community. These groups often offer workshops on everything from composting to seasonal planting strategies, which can enhance your gardening skills and introduce you to like-minded individuals.

Community gardens are particularly beneficial if you don't have space for a garden at home. They provide a plot of land you can cultivate and the chance to contribute to a larger community project. Many community gardens also donate part of their harvest to local food banks, providing a way for you to give back to your community through your gardening efforts.

The shared experience of growing food creates a bond among members in both gardening clubs and community gardens. There's something inherently communal about working alongside others, tending the soil, and sharing the fruits of your collective labor. These interactions can be especially meaningful in retirement, as they provide a sense of purpose and a means to stay active and engaged with others. Whether you're exchanging tips on tomato cultivation or sharing a harvest with neighbors, the social aspects of gardening can add a rich layer of enjoyment to this already rewarding activity.

8.2 BIRD WATCHING IN YOUR LOCAL AREA

The gentle art of bird watching—or **birding,** as it's affectionately known—opens up a world of colorful wings, melodic calls, and the quiet thrill of spotting a rare species. It's a hobby that requires little more than patience and a keen eye, yet it offers rich rewards. If you've never held a pair of binoculars with the intent of spotting a feathered friend, you're in for a delightful surprise.

Bird watching is surprisingly simple to start. First, equip yourself with a basic pair of binoculars, your window to the world of birds. A good beginner's pair doesn't have to be expensive; look for something lightweight with a comfortable grip and good optical clarity. Once you have your binoculars, familiarize yourself with their use—practice focusing quickly and learning how to adjust the diopter, which compensates for differences between your eyes.

Identifying birds is the next step. Start with a good field guide that covers the bird species in your area. These guides provide pictures and descriptions, which will help you distinguish one bird from another. Many also include information on bird calls, which can be just as helpful as visual identification. To enhance your learning, numerous apps are available that help identify birds, log your sightings, and connect you with a community of birdwatchers. Start by observing the most common birds in your area. Pay attention to their size, color patterns, behaviors, and habitats. Over time, your skills will sharpen, and you'll start recognizing species at a glance or by their songs and calls.

Bird watching also brings considerable benefits to your mental and physical health. The act of focusing on birds and their environment helps enhance your attention to detail and can significantly improve your patience and focus. This concentration can be a form of mindfulness, which reduces stress and promotes a peaceful state of mind. Birding might involve walking, sometimes over uneven terrain, which is a great way to boost your cardiovascular health and gently improve mobility. The quiet, repetitive nature of the activity can be very meditative, providing a wonderful escape from the hustle and bustle of daily life.

Joining a bird-watching group or club can improve your experience. These groups often organize guided walks, which are fantastic for beginners. You get to learn from more experienced birdwatchers, and these walks are also an excellent opportunity to explore new areas. Many clubs offer workshops on bird photography or understanding bird behavior, which can deepen your appreciation and knowledge of birding. To find a club near you, check local nature centers, wildlife organizations, or online platforms dedicated to birding. These communities are usually very welcoming to newcomers and can provide a wealth of knowledge and experience.

Creating a bird-friendly environment in your garden or balcony can bring the birds directly to you. Start by installing a bird feeder, which can attract a variety of species. Different types of feeders and food can attract different birds. For example, tube feeders with sunflower seeds are great for finches and titmice, while suet feeders might attract woodpeckers and nuthatches.

A water source, such as a birdbath, can also draw birds to your yard. To make your space more inviting, consider planting native plants and flowers, which offer natural food sources and nesting materials. Not only does this help the local bird population thrive, but it also allows you to observe a range of bird species up close, right from the comfort of your home.

8.3 THE ART OF TEA AND COFFEE TASTING

Exploring Different Varieties

Visualize a quiet morning where the only decision you have to make is whether to start your day with a robust cup of coffee or a delicate tea. Both coffee and tea come with their own unique histories and flavors, making them more than just beverages— they're experiences.

When exploring the world of tea, you encounter varieties like green, black, white, and oolong, each with distinct processing methods and flavor profiles. Green tea, known for its fresh, sometimes grassy flavors, undergoes minimal oxidation, preserving its natural antioxidants. Black tea, on the other hand, is fully oxidized, which results in a darker brew and a richer flavor. As for coffee, the two primary types you'll find are Arabica and Robusta, with Arabica being more widespread, offering a wider range of flavors from sweet-soft to sharp-tangy, depending on its origin and how it's brewed.

Sampling these varieties can be a delightful adventure. Start by visiting local coffee roasters and tea shops, where you can often find samples and flights of different brews. Pay attention to the origin of each variety, as the environment where the tea leaves or coffee beans were grown can significantly influence their taste. For instance, coffee from Ethiopia is famed for its complex, fruity flavors, while Darjeeling tea is often referred to as the "champagne of teas" for its delicate and floral aroma. As you try different samples, note what flavors and characteristics stand out to you—this will help you refine your palate and discover your preferences.

Hosting Tasting Events

Hosting a tea- or coffee-tasting event is a fabulous way to share your newfound knowledge and enthusiasm with friends and family. To start:

1. Choose a theme for your tasting event—perhaps an exploration of Asian teas or a journey through South American coffees. This theme can guide your selection of beverages and help you create a cohesive experience.
2. When preparing for the event, ensure you have a variety of teas or coffees ready for tasting.
3. Provide small cups so guests can try several types without becoming too full or overly caffeinated.

To enhance the tasting experience, pair your chosen teas or coffees with appropriate snacks. Light pastries or biscuits can complement tea flavors, while chocolates or nuts can bring out the depth of coffee. Set up a cozy, inviting environment with comfortable seating and some background music to keep the atmosphere relaxed and enjoyable. During the event, encourage your guests to discuss the flavors they detect and share their thoughts on each brew. This makes the experience more interactive and helps everyone learn from each other's palates.

Health Benefits

While tea and coffee flavor profiles and cultural histories are fascinating, their health benefits are equally compelling. Tea, particularly green tea, is renowned for its antioxidants, which can help reduce the risk of heart disease and cancer. Herbal teas, such as chamomile or peppermint, offer their own health benefits, including aiding digestion and promoting relaxation. Coffee, not to be outdone, has been shown to have potential health benefits, including lowering the risk of type 2 diabetes and offering protective effects on the liver.

However, moderation is key when enjoying these beverages. Too much caffeine can lead to restlessness, anxiety, and disrupted sleep patterns, especially if consumed later in the day. For those sensitive to caffeine, decaffeinated versions of coffee and herbal teas can be good alternatives that allow you to enjoy the ritual and flavor without the stimulating effects.

Learning from Experts

To deepen your understanding and appreciation of tea and coffee, consider attending workshops offered by local tea shops or coffee roasters. These sessions can provide insights into the art of brewing the perfect cup, from the grind size of coffee beans to the temperature and steeping time for tea. Experts can also teach you about the impact of different brewing methods, such as the bold richness of French press coffee or the clean, precise flavors extracted by an AeroPress.

In addition to workshops, many tea and coffee enthusiasts enjoy tours of local roasteries or tea plantations, which can be an enlightening part of your culinary education. These tours often include tastings and discussions with the producers, giving you a firsthand look at the craftsmanship that goes into each cup. Whether standing in the middle of a coffee plantation or a cozy shop with a seasoned barista, each learning experience enriches your understanding and appreciation of these complex and beloved beverages.

8.4 REDISCOVERING LOCAL LIBRARIES

Stepping into your local library can open a treasure trove of resources that go far beyond the rows of books. Modern libraries have transformed into vibrant community hubs where you can attend workshops, enjoy movie nights, and access a wide array of digital media. These institutions are evolving, embracing the role of community centers where knowledge, culture, and technology merge to enrich your life. Imagine participating in a workshop where you learn to paint, attending a lecture that dives deep into local history, or enjoying a classic film with neighbors. These experiences are enriching and foster a sense of community and connection.

Libraries today offer an impressive range of services that cater to diverse interests and needs. For instance, many libraries provide access to digital media platforms where you can download or stream music, movies, and e-books. This digital access is particularly beneficial if you find reading physical books challenging due to vision impairments. Audiobooks, available through library digital services, can be a fantastic way to enjoy literature without straining your eyes. E-books allow for adjusting font size and background color, making reading a pleasure again. Utilizing these resources is typically as simple as logging in with your library card number, and librarians are always ready to help you navigate these new technologies.

The opportunity to volunteer at your local library might be one of the most rewarding aspects of rediscovering this community resource. Libraries often seek volunteers for various roles, from helping with book sales to organizing community events. Volunteering can provide a meaningful way to give back to the community while connecting with people of all ages and backgrounds. Whether shelving books or leading a storytime for children, the time you spend volunteering at the library can help forge new friendships and deepen your connection to your community. It also offers a sense of purpose, contributing to your well-being and happiness.

Libraries are also invaluable as lifelong learning centers. Many offer language learning programs, which can be accessed either in the library or from home. These programs often include a range of languages, accommodating beginners to advanced learners, and sometimes even the opportunity to practice with native speakers.

Additionally, libraries provide access to various educational databases. Whether you want to research genealogy, learn about new medical treatments, or get help with technology, these resources can be accessed with the help of skilled librarians who guide you through the learning process. This access to information supports ongoing education and personal development, making the library a gateway to knowledge and new skills at any stage of life.

As you explore the evolving world of your local library, you'll likely discover that it offers much more than you imagined. From being a quiet place to read and reflect to becoming a lively center of learning and connection, the library can play a pivotal role in enriching your retirement years. So next time you think about heading out for a new adventure, consider your local library. It might surprise you with its offerings, becoming a favorite spot to learn, connect, and contribute.

8.5 THE JOY OF MODEL BUILDING

Imagine dedicating a quiet afternoon to assembling a miniature world where every tiny component is a testament to your dedication and craft. Model building, a hobby that spans generations and interests, offers a satisfying retreat into a world where precision leads to stunning displays of trains, airplanes, and ships. Each type of model building brings its unique flavor and challenges, appealing to different interests and skills.

Model trains, for example, are not just about the locomotives—they're about creating entire landscapes. Enthusiasts often build detailed tracks through miniature towns and countryside scenes, complete with stations, tunnels, and bridges. The appeal lies in both the mechanics of the trains and the creativity of scene-setting.

Airplane models, on the other hand, attract those fascinated by aviation history and the intricacies of aircraft design. From World War II fighters to modern commercial jets, each model is a lesson in aerodynamics and history, captured in scaled-down perfection.

Ship modeling, from historic sailing ships to modern navy vessels, offers a deep dive into maritime history and the complex structures of ships. This type of modeling often involves intricate craftsmanship, as the models include tiny details like rigging, decking, and even interior rooms.

Engaging in these activities hones more than your crafting skills; it develops patience and precision, as each model requires careful assembly and attention to detail. The problem-solving skills you cultivate while figuring out how to fit the tiny pieces together or fix a misalignment are invaluable, spilling over into daily life challenges. The meticulous nature of the work is meditative, allowing you to lose yourself in the task and emerge feeling accomplished and relaxed.

For those looking to share their passion and learn from others, model-building clubs and online forums are treasure troves of resources and camaraderie. These communities are found in most towns and cities and welcome both novices and seasoned builders. Within these groups, you can find workshops and build nights, where members gather to work on projects together, exchange tips, and showcase their latest creations. Online forums offer a platform to share photos of your models, receive feedback, and discuss techniques and new releases in the modeling world. These interactions can be enriching, offering social connections and a wealth of collective knowledge.

Displaying your completed models can be as satisfying as building them. Your home can showcase your models as works of art, each telling a story of the effort and care that went into its creation. You can set up display cases or shelves in a living room or study, where visitors can admire the models that serve as conversation starters.

Lighting plays a crucial role in how these models are viewed. Subtle lighting can highlight the details and craftsmanship of each piece. For a more interactive display, consider setting up a working model train set in a dedicated space, where the trains can run through the scenic tracks, providing dynamic decor. Integrating your models into your home environment creates a living gallery of your achievements, a daily reminder of your skills and passions.

In the realm of model building, the possibilities are as vast as your imagination. Whether it's the joy of watching a model train navigate through a carefully crafted landscape, the pride in perfectly replicating a historical ship or the satisfaction of assembling a complex airplane model, this hobby offers a fulfilling blend of history, engineering, and artistry. It's a pursuit that beautifies your living space and enriches your life with continuous learning and a sense of connection to a community of like-minded enthusiasts. So why not start that model kit you've been eyeing? It could be the beginning of a beautiful adventure in creativity and craftsmanship.

8.6 PHOTOGRAPHY WALKS IN NATURE

Imagine walking through a lush forest or a serene park, camera in hand, ready to capture the fleeting moments that nature generously offers. Planning a successful photography walk involves a bit of preparation, but the rewards are immensely fulfilling.

Start by selecting a location that is picturesque and matches the type of photography you're interested in. Local nature reserves, botanical gardens, or nearby parks can provide diverse photographic opportunities, from sweeping landscapes to intricate floral close-ups. Timing is crucial—early morning or late afternoon, known as the 'golden hours,' offer the best natural lighting for photography. During these times, the soft, diffused light enhances colors and minimizes harsh shadows.

When packing for your photography walk, keep it light but versatile. A good quality camera is, of course, essential. Whether it's a high-end DSLR, a compact mirrorless camera, or even a smartphone, choose a device you are comfortable with. Consider bringing a variety of lenses; a wide-angle lens for landscapes and a macro lens for close-ups of plants and insects can transform your photos. Remember to pack extra batteries and memory cards. A tripod can also be handy, especially if you're interested in experimenting with long exposures or ensuring sharpness in your macro photography.

Techniques in nature require an eye for detail and a sense of creativity. For landscape photography, focus on composition—a well-placed tree, river, or mountain can create a natural flow in the image that leads the viewer's eye through the scene. Wildlife photography, on the other hand, demands patience and a quick trigger finger to capture animals in action. Here, understanding animal behavior and being ready at the right moment is key.

Macro photography offers a portal into a smaller universe, where insects or flowers become the stars of the show. Here, focusing accurately is imperative—even a slight movement can throw your subject out of focus. Adjust your aperture settings to get the desired depth of field: a wider aperture (a lower f-number) for a single subject focus with a blurred background or a narrower aperture (a higher f-number) for more depth and detail throughout the scene.

Embracing mindfulness during your photography walk can significantly enhance both the experience and the outcome. This approach involves being fully present in the moment, absorbing the beauty around you, and reflecting it through your photography. Observe the light, the sounds, and the smells; let them guide your senses to your next subject. This mindful practice not only helps in capturing emotionally powerful images but also makes the activity a meditative process, enriching your connection with nature.

Sharing and documenting your experiences can add a rewarding social element to your photography. Social media platforms offer a space to share your images and engage with a community of photography enthusiasts. This can provide valuable feedback and new ideas, helping you grow as a photographer. Additionally, consider starting a personal blog where you can narrate the stories behind your photographs or even print your favorite images for a personal exhibition at home or a local cafe. These activities allow you to share your passion with others and celebrate your journey and achievements in photography.

In wrapping up this chapter on Finding Joy in Everyday Activities, we've explored how simple pleasures like gardening, bird watching, and photography can profoundly enliven your retirement years. These activities provide gateways to new learning experiences, deeper connections with nature, and the joy of sharing these passions with others. As we move forward, remember that each day offers a new opportunity to explore, create, and connect, turning every ordinary moment into something extraordinary.

CONCLUSION

As we draw the curtains on this journey together through *Your Ultimate Retirement Adventure*, I want to take a moment to appreciate the paths we've explored—from the digital landscapes of modern technology to the vibrant tapestry of social connections. We've dived into the refreshing pools of active living, savored the rich flavors of arts and creativity, and ventured into the ever-expanding horizons of travel and exploration. Along the way, we've embraced the continuous journey of lifelong learning and nurtured our health and well-being, all essential ingredients for a joyful and fulfilling retirement.

Reflecting on our discussions, it's clear that retirement is not just a phase to relax but a significant opportunity to engage deeply with the world in ways we might not have imagined while in the workforce. By embracing technology, we stay connected to our loved ones and the evolving pulse of the world around us.

Staying physically active opens doors to health and vitality, while travel and exploration rekindle the spark of adventure and curiosity.

Lifelong learning keeps our minds sharp and engaged, and arts and creativity offer a powerful outlet for expression and personal growth. Building social connections helps combat loneliness, and maintaining our health ensures that we enjoy these years to their fullest potential.

Retirement is truly transformative—a beginning, not an end. It's a time ripe with opportunities for growth, adventure, and happiness. A chance to reinvent yourself, take on new roles, learn, and explore. As you stand on this wonderful threshold, I encourage you to step forward enthusiastically and confidently. Apply the ideas and activities we've discussed. Venture out of your comfort zone, try new things, and open yourself up to all the possibilities this stage of life offers.

Thank you sincerely for joining me on this exploration. I hope you find joy and fulfillment in your retirement and feel inspired to embark on your own adventure. I encourage you to approach each day with optimism and to share your new experiences and stories with others. Doing so contributes to a vibrant community of active, engaged, and joyful retirees.

As you move forward, I leave you with a question to ponder: What is one new activity or hobby you can start this week that might just become your new passion? Remember, the best time to plant a tree was twenty years ago. The second best time is now.

Here's to your ultimate retirement adventure—may it be filled with curiosity, learning, and a wealth of joy. Happy exploring!

Did you enjoy reading this book and did you already leave a review? Great, thank you!

If not: **YOU CAN MAKE A DIFFERENCE.**

Make the next fellow retiree happy and recommend this book by leaving a useful review on the book's Amazon page, here is the link:

https://www.amazon.com/review/review-your-purchases/?asin=B0DFJ3CXD4

OR

simply scan the QR code to get there:

Your review could mean the world to the next person, significantly contributing to their happiness.

Thank you wholeheartedly in advance!

I wish you all the best in your wonderful post-work life.

Alan Turner

REFERENCES

1. 56 DIY home decor ideas for instant personality. (n.d.). Good Housekeeping. https://www.goodhousekeeping.com/home/decorating-ideas/g1711/diy-home-decor/

2. Aging masterfully. (n.d.). American Libraries. https://americanlibraries-magazine.org/?p=123713

3. A quick guide to starting a blog as a senior. (n.d.). Autumn View Gardens. https://www.autumnviewgardensellisville.com/blog/a-quick-guide-to-starting-a-blog-as-a-senior

4. Benefits of meditation for seniors and apps to help you get started. (n.d.). The Bristal. https://blog.thebristal.com/benefits-of-meditation-for-seniors-and-apps-to-help-you-get-started

5. Best free walking apps of 2024. (n.d.). Verywell Fit. https://www.very-wellfit.com/best-walking-apps-3434995

6. Best phones for seniors in 2024. (n.d.). PCMag. https://www.pcmag.com/picks/the-best-phones-for-seniors

7. Best senior volunteer programs abroad. (n.d.). IVHQ. https://www.volunteerhq.org/senior-volunteers/

8. Best vacation ideas and destinations for seniors. (n.d.). Frommer's. https://www.frommers.com/slideshows/848278-best-vacation-ideas-and-destinations-for-seniors

9. Birding for beginners. (n.d.). U.S. National Park Service. https://www.nps.gov/articles/birding-for-beginners.htm

10. Budget travel guide for seniors: Exploring without breaking the bank. (n.d.). Memory Cherish. https://memorycherish.com/budget-travel-guide/

11. Community engagement strategies for isolated seniors. (n.d.). Nautilus Senior Home Care. https://www.nautilusshc.com/blog/community-engagement-for-seniors

12. ConnectSafely. (n.d.). The senior's guide to online safety. https://connect-safely.org/seniors-guide-to-online-safety/

13. Dance exercise classes for seniors. (n.d.). Silver Sneakers. https://www.silversneakers.com/blog/video/dance-exercise-classes-for-seniors-dancing-classes/

14. Fees & passes - Independence National Historical Park. (n.d.). U.S.
    National Park Service. https://nps.gov/inde/planyourvisit/fees.htm

15. Fees & reservations - Fort Donelson National Battlefield. (n.d.). U.S.
    National Park Service. https://www.nps.-
    gov/fodo/planyourvisit/feesandreservations.htm

16. Five tips to help you start new hobbies in retirement. (2023, June 16). The
    Conversation. https://theconversation.com/five-tips-to-help-you-start-
    new-hobbies-in-retirement-226764

17. Gardening for health: A regular dose of gardening. (n.d.). PMC.
    https://www.ncbi.nlm.nih.gov/pmc/articles/PMC6334070/

18. How to host a potluck, according to experts. (n.d.). Martha Stewart.
    https://www.marthastewart.com/how-to-host-a-potluck-7481945

19. How to host your own tea tasting party. (n.d.). Art of Tea.
    https://www.artoftea.com/blogs/health-lifestyle/how-to-host-your-
    own-tea-tasting-party

20. How to start a water aerobics class in your gym. (n.d.). ASFA.
    https://www.americansportandfitness.com/blogs/fitness-blog/how-to-
    start-a-water-aerobics-class-in-your-gym

21. How to start book clubs for seniors: Your guide. (n.d.). Book Riot.
    https://bookriot.com/book-clubs-for-seniors/

22. Improving chronic disease self-management by older adults. (n.d.). PMC.
    https://www.ncbi.nlm.nih.gov/pmc/articles/PMC5923702/

23. Lifetime senior pass. (n.d.). USGS Store. https://store.usgs.gov/lifetime-
    senior-pass

24. Pottery making for seniors: A fun activity you should try. (n.d.). Wendy's
    Team. https://wendys-team.com/blog-article/pottery-making-for-
    seniors-a-fun-activity-you-should-try/

25. Tai chi for seniors: 3 moves to improve balance and stability. (n.d.).
    Healthline. https://www.healthline.com/health/senior-health/ta-chi

26. The cognitive benefits of lifelong learning for seniors. (n.d.). Knute
    Nelson. https://www.knutenelson.org/news-stories/lifelong-learning-
    benefits

27. The health benefits of knitting. (2016, January 25). The New York Times.
    https://well.blogs.nytimes.com/2016/01/25/the-health-benefits-of-
    knitting/

28. The importance of regular health checkups for seniors. (n.d.). Springfield
    Hospice. https://springfieldhospice.com/the-importance-of-regular-
    health-checkups-for-seniors/

29. Top 5 online learning sites for older adults. (n.d.). Growing Bolder.

https://growingbolder.com/stories/top-5-online-learning-sites-for-older-adults/

30. USDA MyPlate nutrition information for older adults. (n.d.). MyPlate. https://www.myplate.gov/life-stages/older-adults

31. Volunteering and subsequent health and well-being in older adults: An outcome-wide longitudinal approach. (n.d.). PMC. https://www.ncbi.nlm.nih.gov/pmc/articles/PMC7375895/

32. What is digital painting? Your guide to getting started. (n.d.). CG Spectrum. https://www.cgspectrum.com/blog/what-is-digital-painting

33. Yoga for healthy aging: Science or hype? (n.d.). PMC. https://www.ncbi.nlm.nih.gov/pmc/articles/PMC8341166/

Made in the USA
Las Vegas, NV
24 December 2024

15259341R00085